They Will Beat the M

T0274350

"Peter Gelderloos reminds us that for our
memory alive, ensuring that the radical roots ᴏɪ ᴏur movements are not whitewashed by the gatekeepers of history. In remembering, we resist; in forgetting, we
risk erasing our future."

—Franklin Lopez, anarchist filmmaker, founder of subMedia

"A much-needed intervention in this time of profound loss and erasure, *They Will
Beat the Memory Out of Us* is an impassioned counterattack against forgetting. An
inspiring, intergenerational invitation to dig deep for a 'memory of our roots' of
resistance. Woven together from street-smart rebel voices, Gelderloos's book is a
powerful read from start to finish."

—Cindy Milstein, editor of *Constellations of Care: Anarcha-Feminism in Practice*

"Once again, Peter Gelderloos offers us an important book coming from the frontlines of numerous struggles. A must-read for all aspiring trouble makers and those
wanting to free themselves from the grips of exploitation and state terrorism."

—Xander Dunlap, Research Fellow at Boston University
and author of *This System is Killing Us*

"Maintaining and sharing revolutionary love, we strengthen intergenerational
memories of creative resistance. Despite the beatings and burnings meted out
by states, schools, corporations, police, prisons, and militaries, our communities continue to weave overlapping concentric circles of care and resistance. This
striking book reveals collective memories of freedom struggles, despite attempts to
blur, distort or steal our inheritance."

—Joy James, editor of *Beyond Cop Cites: Dismantling State and
Corporate-Funded Armies and Prisons*

"A bold, eloquent, and timely account of the powerful role collective memory plays
in toppling the lies that uphold structures of injustice and inequality. Gelderloos brings into sharp relief the urgency of building social movements that have
continuity and intergenerational memory. The social movement novice and the
seasoned veteran alike will find this book a useful tool to think with."

—Tariq D. Khan, author of *The Republic Shall Be Kept Clean:
How Settler Colonial Violence Shaped Antileft Repression*

"As more and more people are mobilizing against war, genocide, poverty, and
extraction, this book is right on time. Gelderloos' decades of participating in and
studying resistance movements grounds this book's practical analysis of common
misunderstandings cultivated by liberals to stifle resistance efforts. This book
shows the costs—to our boldness, our effectiveness, our solidarity, our survival—
of forgetting lessons learned in our struggles. A much needed tool for the difficult
times we are in and the worse ones that are coming."

—Dean Spade, author of *Mutual Aid*

the future was our skin and now we don't dream any more
—The Tallest Man on Earth

as stars continue
may it continue
—Diane di Prima

Clear water
and centenary olive trees.
Through the alleys,
masked men
and in the towers,
weather-vanes turning.
Eternally
turning.
—Federico García Lorca

They Will Beat the Memory Out of Us

Forcing Nonviolence on Forgetful Movements

Peter Gelderloos

Dedicated to the fighters, the healers, the guides,
and the storytellers

First published 2024 by Pluto Press
New Wing, Somerset House, Strand, London WC2R 1LA
and Pluto Press, Inc.
1930 Village Center Circle, 3-834, Las Vegas, NV 89134

www.plutobooks.com

British Library Cataloguing in Publication Data
A catalogue record for this book is available from the British
Library

ISBN 978 0 7453 4977 0   Paperback
ISBN 978 0 7453 4978 7   PDF
ISBN 978 0 7453 4979 4   EPUB

This book is printed on paper suitable for recycling and made from
fully managed and sustained forest sources. Logging, pulping and
manufacturing processes are expected to conform to the environmental standards of the country of origin.

Typeset by Stanford DTP Services, Northampton, England

Simultaneously printed in the United Kingdom and United States
of America

Contents

CHAPTER 1

They Will Police Us Until We Think It's Normal

The police murder. The police torture. The police rape. The police lie to lock us up in jail and they lie to avoid consequences. The police don't have an especially dangerous job, though they tap into a well funded propaganda machine to portray themselves as heroes. The police were created to uphold a class-based and white supremacist system. The police are infused with a culture that is misogynist, homophobic, and transphobic. The police engage in political repression against those they identify as enemies of a conservative social order. All of these things are true. All of these things have always been true, for as long as the police have existed. All of these things remain true, even when a cop is Black, or a woman, or gay, or grew up poor.

And yet ...

It took us a long time to be able to proclaim these truths openly. Many of us were taught that the police were there to protect us, and all of us have grown up understanding *that* was the *normal* point of view. Those who grew up on the other side of lines of race, class, mental health, sexuality, gender identity, citizenship ... were taught to avoid the cops. If we couldn't take it any longer, we were taught that the next step was to support reform campaigns. More Black cops and women cops,

cops with Pride flags. More reform bills and citizen oversight committees. Because there have never been Black cops and judges before, right? Past reform bills didn't go far enough, oversight committees with teeth haven't been tried yet. Right? But once we make these changes, the problem will finally be solved. Right?

Would the cops have framed my friend if they'd gotten racial sensitivity trainings? Would they have tried to run us over with their vans at that protest if there had been an oversight board? When I was having a depressive episode, would that cop still have threatened to shoot me if only he'd been given a course on dealing with mental health crises? And yet, when I look it up, that city already had an oversight board. In that year, racial sensitivity trainings were already mandatory. Both of those reforms were responses to earlier waves of protest and outrage. All of those facts are there, for anyone to find. And still, this persistent impulse towards reform.

Why don't we know these things?

Why don't we remember?

The Spark

One more push and we were running up the on-ramp. We'd taken the highway! The interstate crisscrosses this part of town like chains, industrial bridges that put a ceiling on any aspirations the neighborhood might have.

The police had been dogging us the whole march, but we stayed together, we kept moving, we got past them, and now the highway was ours. Traffic would stop, commerce would stop, the bullshit would stop. We had declared that normality was abolished, at least for today: we put a stop to it through the force of our protest, our decision to embrace illegality. What made it possible were the meager weapons we had on us, the abundant solidarity, and what felt—at the time—like a limitless determination that things had to change, radically and permanently.

The police had killed someone. Again. We were showing that it's unacceptable to obey the killers, to stay quiet, to look the other way. We were proving to ourselves that we could be strong, that an attack against one of us is an attack against all of us.

This time, the police murder hadn't even happened in our city, not even in our state. The name on our lips was that of a young Black man whose life had been stolen from him on the other side of the country. And here we were starting a riot to mourn him, the most articulate way of expressing that the police are the same everywhere and that we will not dialogue with this system because the only response that is conducive to mourning and healing and rebuilding is to burn it to the ground. The only meaningful thing it can contribute to this new world we have in our hearts is its ashes.

We left the peaceful protest in the park so they could keep on saying a whole lot of nothing. Signing up dupes for their mailing lists. Collecting donations for their board members. We strolled up to the nearest police station to spray their windows, flaunting the impotence of their porcine glares. Going from sidewalks to streets. Visiting gentrifying businesses, redecorating. Swelling in numbers as kids from the neighborhood saw what we were doing and decided, at least for today, we were their people. Getting a police escort and pushing them back. Shrinking a little as some people made their own legit decisions about risk level. Growing again as other people made opposite and equally legit decisions about the kind of risks *they* wanted to assume. And then we

got to that highway on-ramp, and we realized we were
strong enough to take it.

Many readers will assume this account is from 2020, when
the uprisings in response to the police killing of George Floyd
began to spread across the United States. Actually, it's from
six years earlier. Mike Brown had been murdered by cops
in Ferguson, Missouri, on the 9th of August, 2014, leading
to a week and a half of intense rioting around St. Louis. In
November, when the state decided not to prosecute the cop,
rioting broke out again, and this time it spread to multiple
cities across the country. In at least half the cities, police, politicians, and would-be protest leaders succeeded in pacifying
the response in the streets.

But the fact that people remained uncontrollable in so
many other cities is crucial. It was possibly the first time in
the US since the late '60s that an antiracist, anti-police rebellion had spread to that extent. When a revolt spreads as it
did following events in Ferguson, it is a sign of *generalization*. Generalization is the process of riots or revolts becoming
insurrections. In an insurrection, an entire country or region
is engulfed in resistance and struggle. And the transformation
doesn't only manifest in our ability to take over the streets, but
also in our ability to question the assumptions under which
we've been living our entire lives. Most people begin to adopt
critiques that get to the very roots of oppression, they begin
to adopt a revolutionary view of the future, and they begin to
support or even adopt, innovate, and repurpose the forceful
and illegal tactics of sabotage, self-defense, and counterattack
that previously only tiny groups of radicals had engaged in.
Generalization is when large swathes of a society stop looking
at the world around them through the eyes of power, prioritizing the needs of the State to protect itself, and they start

looking at the world with their own eyes, prioritizing their collective needs for survival as members of living communities.

By 2020, after the police murdered George Floyd and the revolt generalized, support for rioting and awareness that the police are a racist institution became *majority* positions for a few weeks,[1] before the media got things back under control.

This process of generalization, of insurrection opening up a revolutionary horizon, is described in the final chapter of the underground book *Here at the Center of the World in Revolt*, written about ten years before the 2020 uprising. That book, already largely forgotten, was not a prediction so much as a memory. Just as we saw a clear resemblance between anti-police rebellions in 2014 and in 2020, there are dynamics in these movements that have happened again and again, year after year, generation after generation.

The first pattern we have to name is that feeling so many of us experience the moment we realize how history rhymes and resonates, that horrifying, liberating moment when we say to ourselves, *this has happened before.* If this has happened before, why didn't we know about it? Did we forget? Did our elders forget without ever telling us?

If we dig deep into our shared past, if we pay attention to how easily we can turn our backs on our own experiences, if

---

1 According to the Gallup poll published in July 2020, two-thirds of people in the US supported the ongoing protests and one in ten had participated, with that number surpassing one in four for young adults. According the Pew Research Center's report on June 12, 2020, an almost identical number, 67 percent, supported the Black Lives Matter movement (which at the time was the catch-all term the media were using to refer to the protests across the country, and not necessarily the NGO of the same name). And according to a *Guardian* poll from July 8, 2020, nine in ten Americans shared the movement's view that police racism and violence were problems, with strong majorities calling them "serious problems."

we ask those who came before us, we may discover that the source of our forgetting is wrapped up with the battles we fight, just as the spark of memory is entangled with the collective learning that comes with resistance.

Already we are forgetting how powerful we were when we began rising up against the oppressiveness of the police in cities across the world. And we weren't just responding to a single issue, we were making connections that broke through borders, like when we shut down hundreds of US airports to stop mass deportations ordered by Trump in 2017.[2] Many people may never learn the steps we took to walk from a reality of total pacification, in which the police and military were murdering people every day without any audible complaint, to a reality in which we were toppling governments, kicking the police out of entire neighborhoods, and winning the space to cultivate healthy, dignified lives.

Veteran of the Black liberation movement and former prisoner Lorenzo Kom'boa Ervin reminds us how:

> […] in the spring of 1992, we saw a massive revolt in Los Angeles, whose immediate causes were related to the outrageous acquittal of four Los Angeles policemen who had brutally beaten Rodney King, a Black civilian. But there again, this was just an immediate cause acting as a trigger; this revolt was not a sympathy revolt for Rodney King personally. The cause of this rebellion was widespread social inequality in the capitalist system and years of police terrorism. This time the rebellion spread to 40 cities and four foreign countries. And it

2   A small portion of these shutdowns are documented in Crime-thInc, "Don't See What Happens, Be What Happens: Continuous Updates from the Airport Blockades," January 29, 2017.

was not just a so-called "race riot," but rather a class revolt that included a large number of Latinos, whites and even Asians. But it was undeniably a revolt against racial injustice first and foremost, even if it was not just directed at white people in general, but the capitalist system and the rich.[3]

Ten thousand US troops were sent in to wage war against the people of Los Angeles. Sixty-three people were killed, nearly 3,000 injured, and 12,000 arrested. I saw the televised riots as a kid. Just eight years later, I was meeting other anarchists for the first time and we talked about '92. We all knew people in LA had been right to fight back against the police, but we didn't know the stories of interracial solidarity, nor did we know that the protests spread to dozens of other cities and jumped borders. Even Black friends and comrades from my generation, unless they specifically grew up in LA, have only a tenuous familiarity with that uprising. What would it take for those stories to be recovered and communalized? And what mechanisms, what forms of violence, kept those stories from spreading farther in the first place?

In a way, the LA riots of '92 were the final epilogue of the Black Liberation movement of the '50s, '60s, and '70s, and an early prologue to the waves of rebellion that have broken in recent years. The level of repression was a testament to how the ruling class saw the people of the city as existing *outside of society*. And their rebellion was an expression of the buried lesson of their predecessors' struggle: the failure of nonviolence.

We all grow up learning the official history: that the movement won civil rights by using nonviolence in the '50s and '60s. They don't explain why the movement continued to

---

3   Lorenzo Kom'boa Ervin, *Anarchism and the Black Revolution*, p.166.

grow in the years after its supposed victories. And nowadays, with radical movements growing again, barely a year passes without Hollywood pumping hundreds of millions of dollars into some new movie or TV show that references Birmingham, the civil disobedience campaign of 1963 that finally forced the desegregation of the South and the passage of the Civil Rights Act. I have yet to come across any mainstream media that portray the true history: in Birmingham, the local population gave up on nonviolence when they saw how ineffective and disempowering it was, they rioted, defeated the cops, and torched every single white business in the city's downtown. Nor do they mention how even many nonviolent campaigners—including King—practiced armed self-defense.

Instead, the official histories turn the entire movement into a simplistic morality play between the discerning, persevering nonviolence of Martin Luther King Jr. and the radical brashness of Malcolm X. For starters, as an older friend who lived through it firsthand reminds us, these movements were much more diverse, but "some of the most egalitarian and anti-authoritarian aspects of the civil rights movement, such as those in which Ella Baker and other women took part, are shunted aside." Just as alarmingly, it turns out that the whole rivalry between King and Malcolm X was fabricated. It was recently discovered that Alex Haley, the celebrated Black journalist and writer who published what is probably the most famous interview with King, made up entire passages to paint the picture that King condemned a more radical and forceful approach. Unpublished transcripts reveal that actually King respected Malcolm and saw their paths as complementary: not exclusive nonviolence, but a diversity of methods towards liberation.[4]

---

4   Gillian Brockell, "MLK's Famous Criticism of Malcolm X Was a 'Fraud,' Author Finds," *Washington Post*, May 10, 2023.

But King and Malcolm were both assassinated with police involvement, as were so many other radical voices in the movement. Alex Haley's career took off. Other movement veterans became politicians or wealthy academics, and a white supremacist society was given an opportunity to update itself and erase the past.

Every city hides a similar memory. The Rust Belt city of Cleveland, where I sit now writing these pages, is no exception. In 1964, Black church leaders called off a desegregation campaign, fearing that the conflict had escalated too much. Their decision to cancel the march didn't keep anyone safe though; a white mob that had formed in Little Italy, preparing to attack civil rights marchers, went and attacked the nearest Black neighborhood instead, as police stood by. Four years later, the city had a progressive Black mayor, but his policies did little to offset police and structural violence. After a shootout in July 1968 between a Black nationalist group and police left three dead on either side, the Black neighborhood of Glenville erupted in perhaps the largest riots the city had seen, with several nights of looting and multiple deaths, probably all caused by police or white vigilantes.

The official response to these rebellions was systematic across the entire US. The policies enacted drew from techniques of counterinsurgency deployed in the Global South, and they indelibly affected the politics of race, policing, and urban planning in other countries as well: structural adjustment, mass impoverishment, mass incarceration, and dehumanization of entire populations. At the same time, the culture industry painted a picture of equality or made the entire problem invisible, while the nonprofit industrial complex exploded, promising reform and resources in exchange for pacification. The gulf between the few who could climb the ladder and the many who were left out only widened. The LA riots of '92 were like a reminder that the struggle had not succeeded, and a warning that it would rise again.

Every lineage, every movement history, has a similar inflection point, a coming to terms with its past failures and an indication of new directions. These moments often occurred around the same time: the Zapatista uprising of 1994 plays a similar role with regards to the anticolonial movements before and since. And this is no coincidence.

All of these movements were not separate realities, nor were they ever truly unified as One Big Movement. Rather, they constituted hundreds of interconnected movements that learned from one another, inspired one another, and supported one another. Everyone was there with their own story, fighting for their own needs within a unique history, but the struggle rejected all borders and could not be captured by any identity: it has always been global, transcendent, transformative, without ever being homogenizing.

The Black liberation movement drew from anticolonial movements that pushed further than the earlier workers' revolutions had gone, and in turn it inspired the feminist movement, the reformist sectors of which required a more radical movement of trans people, queers, and sex workers, all of whom radicalized and spread ideas of disability justice while shining a new light on capitalism and the State. And all of these movements are still around today, interacting.

But we don't get taught this history in school.

What we can do, though, is relearn it, by speaking with the elders who lived through it, or finding their words, whatever accounts they left for us. And we can study the mechanisms of forgetting in our own lives. We can resist by telling the stories.

What stories have already been excluded from the official history of the antiracist rebellions that spread across the country in 2014 and 2020? The stories of where they came from? A white supremacist society, after all, is much safer if its subjects believe that resistance movements just appear out of thin air.

In 2005, the US and much of the rest of the world was still in a period of strong economic growth. The system seemed stable, omnipotent. The last big protest movement—against the US invasion of Iraq—had grown rapidly to produce the largest protests in human history, and it had died just as quickly, killed off by the protest leaders who insisted on strict nonviolence. They got their photo ops, their headline-catching numbers, and the protests were completely peaceful almost everywhere. They declared victory. A few weeks later, the US invaded anyway. People went home.

You couldn't find many, after that, who believed in protest. Nonetheless, certain groups of people made *strategic decisions* to take a stand, using the limited resources they had to try to change things. That year, 2005, neo-Nazis organized a provocative march in a Black neighborhood in Toledo, fully protected by police. They spread race-baiting rhetoric and recycled media tropes about gang violence. With conservatives in power and most social movements immobilized by failures or reeling from heavy cases of repression, it was the far Right's time. The easiest thing would have been to step back. Fortunately, at least one lesson from our shared history has been remembered: *never appease fascists and racists. They will never quit unless they are forced to quit.*

Informal networks of Black youth in the neighborhood, Anti-Racist Action, and Toledo anarchists organized to fight back. Five hundred people gathered, compared to a dozen neo-Nazis. Rather than waiting in the peaceful pose of self-righteous martyrs, people recognized that the first shots were already fired centuries ago. They attacked the police, who were the most relevant force of white supremacy on the scene. The police responded with arrests but people didn't abandon the streets, sparking four hours of rioting. Eleven cops were injured, police and media vehicles were attacked, a gas station was looted, and a local bar where cops and politicians often gathered was torched.

The cops were once again collaborating with neo-Nazis, advocating a genocide that wasn't just hypothetical, it was ongoing. But this time, they got punished. Even more importantly, Black youth from dispossessed neighborhoods weren't left alone to fight for their survival, criminalized by the NGOs that claimed to represent them. This time, radicals from other neighborhoods—white, Black, and Brown—decided to make good on their promise of solidarity; they came out into the streets to share the risks, to increase the political costs of police repression, and to support those who got arrested in the riots.

Four years earlier, I remember reading about a riot in another Rust Belt city, Cincinnati, after the police killing of Timothy Thomas. None of us in my region knew whether the folks in Cincinnati had support when they rose up to avenge their friend. From a distance, it seemed like they did not. We knew that a conversation was spreading, and the conclusion was increasingly becoming clear: *since the police will never stop murdering, all of us need to respond. Those who fight back, often the friends and neighbors of the person killed, should never have to face the risks alone.*

These learning processes occurred amidst the highs and lows of other conflicts. After Hurricane Katrina devastated New Orleans in 2005, the police and urban planners came through to inflict an even greater violence. They were evicting, imprisoning, and executing Black people before the storm even subsided. Next, investors and city officials plotted to empty out devastated Black neighborhoods so they could flip the properties and gentrify them in the service of the city's tourism industry. Elders from the Black Liberation movement and anarchists from the city and from farther afield teamed up to create safe spaces where neighbors who had lost their housing could access health care and other vital resources. In the longer term, they helped neighbors to rebuild and move back in. At the center of this solidarity work was an ability to see that fighting back against the police had to go hand-in-hand with building long-term relationships and developing infrastructures and practices of mutual aid, healing, and harm reduction. The popular, self-organized responses to state violence around Hurricane Katrina (and in 2012, Hurricane Sandy) gave us opportunities, for once, to learn from our successes. Unfortunately, there were also major failures we had to learn from fast. We learned that support infrastructures were vulnerable to police infiltration and to authoritarian, abusive personalities. Patriarchal dynamics in our movements make us more vulnerable to both infiltrators and authoritarians. Both of those lessons had already been learned in the antiracist and anticapitalist movements of the '60s and '70s. So why had they been forgotten?

The most vocal veterans of those earlier struggles weren't passing on many useful lessons. Instead, they seemed to be profiting off their status and using the platform given to them by the institutions of power to pacify any future resistance. This certainly seemed to be the case in 2006 when Al Sharpton and his NGO made sure protests in New York City remained completely peaceful—and completely ineffective—after police murdered Sean Bell in a hail of 50 bullets. To be able to effectively resist the police, we would first need to find out how to get around those who made it their jobs to protect the police: the loyal opposition.

Connections on an international level were occurring as well. In 2006, a teachers' strike in the Mexican state of Oaxaca led to a general uprising that pushed out the police and connected issues of impoverishment, police murders, Indigenous resistance, land defense, food justice, and the defense of grassroots culture. Coalescing out of a forceful rebellion against police, whom they identified as agents of colonial capitalism and state power, the movement took on an increasingly revolutionary horizon and anarchist character as people organized themselves through assemblies. It was eventually pacified by authoritarian tendencies pushing for a centralization of the assemblies and for negotiation with the State. But in the meantime, the rebellion and its lessons were spreading internationally. There were protests and solidarity actions in cities across the world, as well as delegates to connect with what was happening on the ground. One US anarchist was killed by paramilitaries on the barricades, together with 26 people from Oaxaca.

Simultaneously, for three months in 2006, millions of young people all over France organized assemblies, held protests, blocked roads, attacked banks, and fought the police in opposition to a strict neoliberal labor law that had been introduced to increase the precarity and exploitation of workers. It is highly unlikely they would have stood up so forcefully, nor used such effective tactics for keeping back the police, if it weren't for the inspiration gained in an anti-police revolt the year before, when racialized youth in impoverished suburbs across the country rose up for three weeks, burning cars and fighting the forces of order after two teenagers died in a police chase.

In 2007, after migrants in the US helped recover a rebellious tradition of strikes and resistance on May Day, largely latine workers on strike in LA started to riot in MacArthur

Park in response to police aggression. A year later in Malmö, Sweden, kids and teenagers from immigrant Muslim families, together with anarchists and radical leftists in Antifascist Action rose up for two nights in response to growing racism and Islamophobia. Police were unable to quell the uprising, and adult Muslims from an affiliated cultural organization had to restore the peace on their behalf. It was the first of several multiracial, antiracist, anti-police, and anti-gentrification uprisings with anarchist participation in Sweden.

And then at the end of 2008, people essentially took over the entirety of Greece for nearly a month, burning almost every single police station and bank in the country, after cops murdered a 15-year-old anarchist in the neighborhood of Exarcheia in Athens. Police were never able to defeat the uprising, and for the next ten years, the State was effectively unable to touch multiple liberated areas in Athens and beyond. To restore their control, the Greek government required a complex counterinsurgency plan with immense support from the European Union, that included police collaboration with growing fascist street movements, the media encouragement of xenophobia and strict new border laws to manufacture an immigration crisis, mass internment and frequent killings of undocumented people, and the deliberate impoverishment of Greek society. Devastating elements of the counterinsurgency plan were carried out by the Left. Capitalizing on the rebellion, the most progressive government postwar Europe had ever seen took power and convinced social movements to support a referendum that effectively rejected neoliberal capitalism. The leftist political party, predictably, refused to carry out their referendum, and between mounting poverty, extreme police violence, and their feelings of betrayal and cynicism, many people gave up.

While it was still unfolding, the 2008 insurrection resonated internationally. Back in the US, people were talking about it, too. And then New Year's Day rolled around—usually a chance for new beginnings, for optimism. Not a day you want to be forced to see that nothing ever changes. The following account comes from *Unfinished Acts*, published by a multiracial group of anarchists from Oakland and San Francisco:

January 1st, 2009. New years day. A Thursday. We hear that a Black man has been shot and killed by a BART (Bay Area Rapid Transit) police officer. People who took video of the incident had their phones and cameras quickly confiscated by the police. He was executed during the first few hours after midnight, while partygoers were on their way home from trying to burn a fond memory into their heads and kick off another time around the sun.

They shot Oscar Grant III in the back. He worked as a butcher at the grocery store where my friend and I shop at every week. When I saw his picture, I recognized his smile.

We were overwhelmed with depression, helplessness. Another Black man killed by cops in the Bay, and nothing being done about it. The general public digests the news with a frown and goes about their business. What cynical cruelty passes as normality. [...]

Somewhere, at some point, our disbelief gave way to rage, to anger, to a clarity of purpose and focus. [...]

We are here, in the plaza by the entrance to the Fruit-vale station, the site of the murder of Oscar Grant, a crowd of approximately 1,000. Our friends are getting off the shuttle. 4pm. There are many banners, many faces: Oakland youngsters, youth-organizers, communists, anarchists, mostly young, and multiracial. The station is closed and the PA is very loud. The rally has now begun.

Speeches are being made from the sound system in the center of the crowd. The emcee is a professional activist: "Listen everybody, we need to get organized and be peaceful, not let our emotions take over."

She's greeted with an enormous silence from the crowd. She continues on, undeterred: "But right now we'd like to open it up to anyone who's ever been harassed by the police—would you like to come up and speak? Especially our youth, feel free to come up right now and tell your story."

Young people begin to take the mic:

I'm feelin pretty violent right now, I'm on some Malcolm X shit: by any means necessary. If I don't see some action, I'm going to cause a ruckus myself.

That's right!

There are cheers and applause, and chants:

No Justice, No Peace! Fuck the Police!

When you get bullied at the playground you don't sit down and beg that fucking bully to leave you alone! You knock his fucking teeth out. We've been bullied for too long, we've been talking too long, we gotta take fucking action, you know what I'm saying? Because you don't get results by pleading to the fucking bully, you beat his fucking ass and you let his ass know that you're not to be fucked with. That's how it goes.

Yes, right on!

Our anonymous narrators relate how the crowd booed a representative of the mayor's office who tries to speak, and how chants for a march spread throughout the crowd. Finally, a large group abandons the peaceful rally and sets off down the street:

[...] young people, communists, anarchists, neo-Black Panthers. All kinds of signs and styles of dress represent their affiliations: the fitteds of hiphop heads, the berets of the Panthers and Brown Berets, Maoists and their ubiquitous paper, anarchists and their all black clothing, but mostly it's Oakland's children: Black and Brown youth. At the front of the march is a crew on their scraper bikes. The march leaves down International Blvd, a thoroughfare that crosses the largely Black and Latin@ Fruitvale neighborhood and the largely Asian Lake Merritt neighborhood. The police presence is light, mostly staying ahead and behind the march clearing traffic. Hundreds of black masks are being handed out; residents and car commuters voice their support. The mood is spontaneous, loud, and unruly: groups of kids run up and down through the march, no one was solemn, tired, or quiet. The mood is electric with anger. [...]

As we move towards the Lake Merritt BART station, people in the crowd chant about BART as the target. Moving off freeways and into the edge of downtown, the frustration begins to feel more focused; we're moving towards BART police headquarters. A young woman lights a bundle of paper on fire and raises it defiantly above her head. As we all move towards the BART station, there's the feeling of moving as a single unit. [...]

Hey there is a dumpster down that block. You guys want to go get it?

What about the cops down there?

They're far away enough that they won't mess with us.

Five people move the dumpster into the crowd and start to bang on it; cheers erupt.

At 8th and Madison a police cruiser is blocking traffic next to BART police headquarters. It becomes the focal point of people's anger as people start to surround it. Two officers get out, noticeably concerned about the angry crowd.

Pigs go home! Pigs go home!

The cops quickly grab whatever they can out of the cruiser and retreat into the lines of backed-up traffic. Young folks emerge from the crowd and start to jump on the police cruiser, kicking and smashing out its windows. A rare moment of cross-racial solidarity sets in as people dance on the cruiser: Latin@s, Black folks, Asians and whites are tearing down well guarded day-to-day boundaries. Owning and making real our shared fury at the police, we find a crucial point of political intersection and act on it.

A masked kid approaches the group around the dumpster on the other side of the street:

Should I spark this shit?

Yeah go for it.

The dumpster catches fire and is passed from hand to hand before being rammed into the police vehicle, which at this point is almost entirely destroyed. The crowd starts to rock the police car trying to overturn it. OPD riot cops who have been gearing up a block away spring into action and advance on the crowd opening fire with tear gas, bean bag rounds and other projectiles. People are yelling and running.

The riot for Oscar Grant has started. What was the role of the Left? They had tried to squash the uprising, to turn it into a peaceful protest, and they failed. A precondition for any kind of resistance or growing rebellion is for people to give up their trust in the professional organizers, the NGOs, the political parties, the churches.

And what was the role of the anarchists? Referring back to *Unfinished Acts*:

The short answer is that their role was minimal. There were some anarchist affinity groups scattered throughout the streets during those days of unrest. A few did travel from afar to lend a hand but the vast majority lived and organized in the Bay Area. Either way, their participation was dwarfed by that of the crews of diverse Oakland youth who animated the rebellion and gave it the fierce energy that made the state tremble.

The longer answer is a bit more complicated and opens up important questions. As soon as the actual riots unfolded, anarchists were relatively insignificant in the outcome of the street battles. But if it were not for their initial actions early on January 7, those riots would most likely not have happened. Anarchists helped instigate and protect the march that broke away from the vigil at Fruitvale BART. They made sure that no group could coopt the anger or pacify the crowd. And when the march reached downtown, it was the actions of a few anarchists that provided an initial spark which led to the first confrontations and the trashing of an OPD cruiser. They then quickly became lost in the crowd as the real anarchy took over and the full potential of the evening unfolded.

A week later, there was another riot. This time, the Left came prepared, with dozens of "peace police," or protest marshals in reflective vests trying to herd the whole rally. But people broke out of those constraints and seized the streets again. Black people led the way, including a couple of Bay Area anarchists who stole the megaphone from one of the would-be leaders.

In the next year, anarchists in medium-sized or even small crowds would start riots after police murders in Portland, Seattle, and Denver. They also carried out illegal attacks at night, starting to give material force to the promise that *for every murder, there will be a response*. The consistency of these actions, the determination, and the accumulation of tactical knowledge, are vital to setting the stage for the huge, country-wide insurrections that will follow a few years later.

There was also a change in popular consciousness. The authors of *Unfinished Acts* talk about how the practice of illegal parties—not political parties but *fun* parties—played into and strengthened the 2009 Oscar Grant Rebellion. In particular, the *sideshows* enabled Bay Area youth targeted by the police to assert how taking over the streets is both liberating and enjoyable. Sideshows, an outgrowth of hip-hop culture originating in Oakland in the '80s, are temporary, illegal occupations of an intersection, where youth perform doughnuts or other stunts in their cars before dispersing. They were a perfect fit for the rebellion, spreading contempt for the law, a strong claim to public space, a celebratory and autonomous culture, and good security practices: do what you came to do, have a good time doing it, and then move on to the next spot before the cops can gather enough strength to crack down, Music culture was also an important feature of the rebellion. *Local* artists were often the ones to contribute the unofficial soundtracks to each new riot. Just to keep pace with the radical sentiments and exciting experiences spreading in the streets, Big Label musicians had to flood their videos with images of riots.

A similar learning process took place in Los Angeles in 2012, after police in Anaheim killed Manuel Díaz, shooting him in the back. Kandist Mallett is a writer and journalist from LA who has been active and present in movement waves since Occupy. She describes the resulting protests: "the fireworks were going off in Disneyland a few blocks away as I was running from the rubber bullets and tear gas." How did the rebellion begin? Readers may notice a pattern: "After a meeting with the city, protests started, someone set a dumpster on fire, ANSWER[5] tried to discourage similar actions, police deployed a huge amount of force but the protest expanded beyond their ability to kettle it."

Police aren't the only ones working to kettle our movements. Kandist describes authoritarian movement leaders fighting a "territorial battle over who gets to ride this wave. LA is a hard place to organize because there are so many groups that are well established and are quick to respond and try to control things." The role of the authoritarian Left to pacify popular responses to rebellion isn't just occasional: "the cooptation is built in."

And yet sometimes, we get stronger. Things seemed to die down quickly after 2012, but really, there was a subterranean process of learning going on. In Kandist's words, "you go into each wave, and you take those experiences with you. The people who participate learn from those experiences, and I'm an example of that":

> In 2013, there was a march for Trayvon Martin. We tried to go from Leimert Park (a predominantly, historically Black neighborhood) to Beverly Hills. Of course the cops wouldn't let us. Fast forward to 2020, and people were rioting and looting in Beverly Hills and Pico and Melrose (all extremely rich neighborhoods). I would not in my wildest dreams have imagined that happening.
>
> Now this was the opposite of cooptation, this was us taking back control of these movements. BLM[6] was

---

5   ANSWER is a vanguardist, mass protest organization with vague politics that functions essentially as a front group created by another front group.

6   "Black Lives Matter" began as a decentralized rallying cry against systematic police murders of Black people. In 2017, however, it was incorporated as an NGO that has since raked in hundreds

trying to hold some march nearby and they lost control of things. It became a riot, and I know that's not what they wanted or intended. People started looting and it became wild. When I think of collective memory, I think of that: each wave, when it happens, is an attempt to push the line further and further.

In 2020, anyone who had experienced the protests for Trayvon Martin or before, they were learning or thinking about what had happened. Those earlier experiences helped the rioting in 2020 to transpire. Even more importantly, people were thinking about '92 (the Rodney King riots). I think '92 was such a strong, powerful event, even if you weren't physically there or you were too young to be there or you weren't even born yet, you understand what happened. People who were on the streets in 2020 were thinking about that. But they were also tuned into the feeling in the air. The fact that people were rioting in Minneapolis and in so many other places, that environment, was a major driving force.

History always feels present in the streets during these rebellions, but it doesn't appear as doctrine. On the contrary, everything can be questioned, challenged, changed. I spoke with my friend Kat, from St. Louis, about how the space that opened up in the streets of the city was a space of learning—learning how to fight back in the face of immense risk:

Mike Brown's body was left in the street for hours, allowing people in the neighborhood to gather, for word

---

of millions of dollars, supported politicians, and given out tens of millions of dollars in payments to friends and family members of the board: https://apnews.com/article/government-and-politics-race-ethnicity-philanthropy-black-lives-matter-5bc4772e029da52 2036f8ad2a02990aa (accessed April 20, 2024).

to spread, and for confrontation and tensions to immediately grow. And there was immediately a forceful, aggressive response by police. But over the following days, people pushed back in a powerful, intensified way. Part of this is due to the sheer amount of police murders in the St Louis area, but honestly people don't usually respond with much vigor or fortitude. The rage was contagious, and people amassed power and agency in the streets from jump—allowing people to believe that fighting back was possible. Part of this was due to ways that people learned to revolt as the week went on— learning to make Molotov cocktails, figuring out how to safely throw the tear gas canisters back, people showing each other how to make masks out of t-shirts and passing out masks to each other. The day after a protester was shot by gunfire meant for the cops, people were shouting, "if you're going to shoot, shoot straight" and encouraging each other not to fire through the crowd. A strong anti-snitch culture across the city and surrounding areas made it near impossible for them to identify looters and rioters from surveillance footage. Part of this was due to the sheer number of guns that people were carrying. This is not to be confused with organized forces of militias or revolutionary power, this was just people personally carrying. The tension that created appeared to fuel a deep hesitancy on the part of the police from simply pushing into the crowds. And multiple people were shot over the course of the first week, some by interpersonal conflict, some in individual criminal confrontation with police, some by stray gunfire meant for the police.

What helped this rebellion flare up again three months later, and this time, to spread across the country, when the state refused to indict the killer cop?

My sense is that it was less about formal organizing efforts and more about an openness of possibility when people saw both what happened in Ferguson/St Louis and what happened in other places. Hope and witness became a catalyst for possibility.

Returning to Charles, our anarchist friend helping a protest turn into a riot in North Carolina in November 2014:

Going up on the elevated highway might not have been the smartest move, tactically. In other cities, cops would turn highway occupations into death traps. Letting far Right drivers through to run over protesters. Charging, so people would jump or fall off the sides trying to get away. This time, though, they didn't want to escalate, and in upping the illegality of our protest, we literally and figuratively rose above the ineffectual police escort, and achieved a new kind of peace.

So many steps had led us to this spot. The family of the young kid the cops had killed in our town earlier in the year were brave: they refused to stay quiet, insisting it was a murder. Then his skateboarder friends and the local anarchists stepped up to support the family, helped them find resources and a platform. (Too often, the family of a victim call for peace after a police murder, and the friends want to fight back but they're never given the same legitimacy. When the riots start, the media keep on saying they're outside agitators going against the wishes of the family.)

The day the news hit that the Ferguson cops weren't being charged, we had that determination we'd built up together. That's what allowed us to turn our backs on the official rally, which was the usual silent protest locked down by the groups who claim to own any movement opposing the police—basically NGOs fronted by the local Black bourgeoisie and kept afloat by wealthy benefactors. They had tried to shut us down when we started loud chants, when we started going in our own direction. I remember the army of white college kids abusing my friend, calling her racist for "not respecting Black leadership" (she's a woman of color). I imagine the "training" those college kids needed to prepare them for this. Getting ingrained in the belief that being a good ally meant not learning anything about the history and debates of Black liberation movements, the fact that there was not one single position. You can't take any action against racism without taking sides in those debates, without choosing a strategy. These college kids probably thought there was one "Black strategy" for opposing racism, one "Indigenous strategy" for opposing colonialism, one "women's strategy" for opposing patriarchy. Or they subconsciously recognized that there *was* a strategy that kept them safer. They never acknowledged their own agency and their own skin in the game. They chose safety and a performance of obedience, following the directives of the spokesperson of the correct demographic with the biggest megaphone. Inevitably, that's a megaphone paid for with white money.

The pacifiers were out in force everywhere, but the news kept trickling in, first in drips and drops, then in a roar. Updates from message boards and news reports and Signal threads, read off of screens and then shouted out in passionate voices in the human space of the riot: in one city after another, people were rising up.

There was wild cheering now. We kept shouting his name, Mike Brown, and the name of Chuy Huerta, and a litany of other names, people the cops stole from us. But the mourning and rage became a celebration. A celebration of their lives, of all life. Of memory. Of the dignity we pluck out of the jaws of this brutalizing system. Of the strength of our resistance.

Some young queer Black and latine kids started dancing. I stayed on the makeshift barricade watching the police, but the beat spread. We were holding a dance party on the highway. This wasn't a government interstate anymore. We had taken this ugly concrete monstrosity and transformed it into exactly what we needed, from one moment to the next.

So many people had said it would be impossible for a large-scale, widespread insurrection to break out in this country. Rebellion could, at most, be localized to one or two cities. Want to know who was right? It wasn't the defeatists. They didn't know what the hell they were talking about, masking their fears in sociology or materialism or that false incrementalism that never seems to arrive at the promised destination.

Do you know who was right about rebellion being possible? It was those of us who *made rebellion possible* through our blood, sweat, and tears, by taking risks, by building up real antiracist relationships and spreading historically grounded critiques of the police and the State in the quiet moments, risking our freedom through acts of sabotage and attack in the moments that shouldn't have been quiet, and putting ourselves in the crosshair, taking the streets—staying smart but going wild—even if we could only get a hundred people together.

I need to say this because it would break my fucking heart if people in struggle forgot this lesson all over again. *We were right*. We discovered a truth that those who came before us, two generations ago, had already discovered. It was a truth that became a secret because that generation was pummeled into the dust—by prison, by police murders, by disease epidemics, by drugs—and because the generation after them failed in their responsibility to life, they failed to gather up all the lessons those who came before them had died for. They turned their backs on all that sacrifice because pacifism or reformism or an NGO paycheck or the dream of striking gold was a smaller risk and paid better dividends. You didn't have to be responsible to your fellow humans, you just had to be an individual, looking out for number 1 (even and especially if you were getting paid to "represent your community" or "bring resources to the disadvantaged").

So what's the truth we rediscovered? Despite the strength of the military and the police, a million people can take over a city. How do a million people rise up?

The secret of a million people rising up is that a thousand people can rise up. The secret of a thousand people rising up is that a hundred people can rise up. The secret of a hundred people rising up is that a single person can rise up. And the truth that a single person and a million people share is that if a single person cannot rise up, a million people are nothing but a herd and they will go whichever way their shepherds tell them to.

We discovered this because some of us found ourselves alone at night with spray paint and a hammer. We discovered this because we responded to police killings when we only numbered a dozen or a hundred and everyone else said it was too risky, it wouldn't change anything. We discovered this because we braved the contradiction that maybe we can criticize other people's fear and inactivity but also empathize with it, build relationships, see people as beings in motion and help them see the choice to change where they're going.

And having walked some version of that path is the only thing that makes us a "we." We have nothing else in common. We don't all know each other. We're not an invisible party. We don't agree on many things. We'll never all be friends. And that's okay. We'll still try to have each other's backs.

What can we learn from this secret? What does it tell us about the times when we push for a broader response, and for a variety of reasons people don't come out into the streets, or they let themselves get pacified and herded around by self-appointed protest leaders? I spoke with one anarchist who agreed to talk on condition of anonymity:

We were a small group. Just the right size. Three lookouts. Two covering either approach, in line of sight with the third, who was by the action. Communicating with laser pointers. No phones—no pocket snitches tracking our movements. Our phones weren't turned off either, that's a flag, and they can use it as evidence of conspiracy. The phones stayed home. No flashlights. A laser pointer doesn't throw off any light unless you're right in the line it's being pointed in. No shouting or whistling that might cause neighbors to look out their windows.

I had a dead phone in my hand. No battery, insides melted. But to anyone who saw me, I was just standing there looking at the screen, which is the least suspicious thing to be doing these days if you're hanging around on a street corner, aside from smoking a cigarette or walking a dog.

We had all practiced a relaxed posture. Not the "crime posture" folks who are new to this always adopt.

And folks who aren't so new to it, but haven't yet separated the adrenaline from the mission. Also, criminals in movies. Criminals in movies always adopt "I'm a mysterious tough guy" posture when they're doing something illegal.

As for the action, that was a few more comrades, breaking into the transformer for the building and putting in a [deleted for legal purposes]. What was the building? Let me just say it was a building directly connected to the police, with a dead angle and no cameras on this one electrical panel.

The police had murdered again, the incorrigible bastards. There had been a weak response in the streets. We wanted to remind people that the night still belongs to them. That they can always find ways to fight back.

The action was quick. I gave a green light to signal "all clear." The other lookout must have too, because our people in the middle got started and in no time they were already walking away. I gave another green to let them know it was still clear on my end, in case they had to change their escape route last minute, and I walked the whole way out of the neighborhood, staying chill, taking a path with minimal cameras. I passed a patrol car at one point. Acted bored and tired, kept walking. Because of our brilliant delay mechanism, it would be a while before any calls were put in to the fire department.

The next day it was in the news. I think it was a million in damages, and the building didn't have any power for a full week.

Most importantly, a lot of people got the reminder: we don't forget.

The person who shared this with me didn't want to give any kind of name, nor identify the city they lived in, and they asked me to make some changes to their wording to throw off the forensic linguists who sometimes work for the police.

It's a reminder that the pacifists and the legalists have an advantage when it comes to imposing their history and drowning out our own: it's dangerous to talk. Some actions never get spoken about after they're carried out, and that's a best-case scenario; someone talking is a danger to everybody. Yet, by protecting ourselves from repression, it's easy to give in to silence. The anonymous author of "Secrets and Lies" reminds us, "All cultures of secrecy come up against problems."[7] Among these: if the histories of our own struggles are lost, so too is the chance to pass on practical wisdom, strategic lessons, the realization that we can actually fight back.

Nonetheless, memory can reemerge, and formidable lies that have stood, not just for a generation or two but for centuries—lies that define an era—can come toppling down.

Statues

On the 7th of June, 2020, a multiracial crowd led by Black youth in Bristol, England, toppled the statue of Edward Colston. The usual commentators on the Right and also some on the Left condemned the so-called "violence" and claimed the destruction of a historical monument was the destruction of history itself.

Who was the bronzed figure at the center of this conflict? Living in the seventeenth and eighteenth centuries, Colston was a merchant, a member of Parliament, and a senior executive in the Royal African Company. Colston dedicated his

---

7 Anonymous, "Secrets and Lies," *325* no.7, October 2009: https://theanarchistlibrary.org/library/anonymous-secrets-and-lies (accessed April 20, 2024).

life to enriching himself by enslaving and trafficking Black people. That was his life's central work. His fellow rich and powerful people esteemed him as a philanthropist and gentleman not *in spite* of him being a slaver, but *because* of it. All of his peers knew that the slave trade was one of the best ways to make money at the time. And they also knew that it was a gruesome, monstrous business. But the rich and powerful, as a rule, have made their peace with acting monstrously.

The wealthy also know that funding hospitals and schools, like Colston did, is a sure way to gain admiration, to indoctrinate the lower classes to adopt their worldview, and to create tools of social welfare—bread and circuses—that are just as vital for maintaining control as having a police force that obeys your commands.

The true erasure of history came in 1895 when Bristol city leaders erected a statue to Colston without naming him as a leading architect and profiteer from the Black genocide. The omission was no coincidence. In the mid-1800s, the UK had abolished slavery, but its colonial empire was still in expansion. To cover up the contradictions, the British ruling class had to portray themselves as the bringers of culture and progress and selling that brand meant erasing the reality of colonialism and eliding the historical source of their wealth, which, in the case of Colston, the Royal Family, and a significant part of the British elite, was human trafficking and forced labor.

The Bristol protesters who threw Colston into the harbor that had once been full of his slave ships stood at an important intersection. They organized their protest as a border-defying show of solidarity with George Floyd: another example of how our struggles resonate globally.

But also—and this is vital—they were building off a very local history of organizing, resistance, and rage. Over the prior decade-and-a-half, people targeted by police violence because of their skin color, their gender expression, their economic class, or their political organizing had become increasingly determined in creating responses. One of the most dramatic examples were the riots that started in Tottenham in north London and spread to several cities across England after the police murdered Mark Duggan on the 4th of August 2011.

In Bristol in particular, lower-class and racialized residents had been dealing with police profiling, racist rhetoric from rightwing politicians, and inflated housing prices that were increasingly pushing people into poverty. In April 2011, protests against the opening of a new Tesco store on Cheltenham Road erupted into riots after police raided a nearby squat. A few months later, Bristol was one of the cities to riot against the murder of Mark Duggan. As the Right aggressively tried to raise the specter of a race war by blaming the problems of capitalism on racialized people and migrants, Bristol became a center of antiracist and antifascist organizing, building an alternative of interracial solidarity amongst the lower classes.

This solidarity was on display in the crowds who toppled Colston, defying police and media attempts to divide them. And what they did was make history, not destroy it. They built the power to take the streets, to reach out and change the world we are forced to live in. And the graffiti-covered plinth they left behind—*sans* Colston—told a much richer and truer story than Colston's bronze statue and fictitious plaque ever had.

Abigail Graham is a mixed-heritage student from London, with family in Bristol. She was at the protest that day:

> I was farther back in the march when Colston was
> thrown into the harbour, however I heard roars of happi-
> ness that passed through the crowd. I remember sitting

in Castle Park afterwards. I had seen the empty plinth when I had walked past, but knowing that the statue was in the river Avon was honestly delightful. There are way too many statues of racist figureheads that are still up in the UK today, but the toppling of Colston set a precedent that this is the start of things really changing for people of colour.

It is too easy to ignore that which doesn't directly impact you, and I feel that the BLM protests really forced white people to think about their actions. Watching the video of Colston being thrown into the harbour the evening of the protest made me feel like people care. It made me feel like the world may be changing.

I am mixed heritage, my father is Black and my mother white. I was lucky enough to have anarchy and antiracism ingrained in the white side of my family. This meant that I always felt acceptance within spaces that they were in. When I went to university I experienced racism relatively frequently—people trying to touch my hair in the street or successfully doing it at the bus station, customers at work discussing how they loved when the Jamaicans (my father's family are Jamaican) came over to help on Windrush and that Blacks are okay but it's the Muslims they can't stand.

History is also whitewashed, like how everyone worships the Suffragette movement for giving women the vote—no one discusses how they gave white women the vote. Similarly to how I am told I have a chip on my shoulder for being angry about the slave trade, when I know my surname is the name that plantation owners gave my ancestors.

It can be quite othering, and it can feel like people are going to scrutinize your every move for speaking out. It is easy to place yourself in an echo chamber on social media, but there are areas I will not go due to racism. I

> cannot change my skin tone when I visit Cornwall. I can
> straighten my hair, but my features are not white. I cannot
> pick and choose when to be perceived as a woman of
> colour, and unfortunately there are people who will judge
> me based on my skin and my skin alone. But knowing
> that there are movements that are trying to stamp this
> out—movements that have white members—gives me
> reassurance that our voices will start to be heard.

Colston's was not the only monument to be toppled. Across the US South, a movement to remove statues celebrating Confederate leaders and defenders of slavery had begun to spread after the Ferguson uprising in 2014 and the Charleston church shooting the next year.[8] But legal, peaceful actions involving petitions and pressure on city councils were easily stalled for years through subcommittees and legal filings. That was the case with the Robert E. Lee and Stonewall Jackson monuments in Charlottesville, Virginia. Entering into the fray, white supremacists organized a major rally on August 11, 2017, to build support for the monuments and spread a message of race war. As the police stood by, they beat antiracist counterprotesters. But many of the antiracists came prepared to fight back, and in a number of clashes beat the white supremacists in the streets. Cornel West, protesting with a group of clergy who were sticking to nonviolent tactics, said "we would have been crushed like cockroaches if it were not for the anarchists and the anti-fascists."[9] The next

8   Debbie Elliott, "5 Years After Charleston Church Massacre, What Have We Learned?," *NPR*, June 17, 2020: www.npr.org/2020/06/17/878828088/5-years-after-charleston-church-massacre-what-have-we-learned (accessed April 20, 2024).
9   Cornel West and Traci Blackmon (August 14, 2017), "Cornel West & Rev. Traci Blackmon: Clergy in Charlottesville Were Trapped by Torch-Wielding Nazis," Interview with Amy

day, however, again with police standing by, one of the white supremacists drove a car through the crowd of counterprotesters, injuring 35 and killing one, Heather Heyer.

In response, two days later, a collection of socialists and anarchists tore down the Confederate statue staring down on Durham, North Carolina. And again, they left the foundation of the monument, graffitied and broken, as a testament to memory, a different kind of monument telling a much more complex history.

And that more complex history requires a more complex relationship with the space we inhabit. To not lose the memory of where we come from, we need to be in constant dialogue with the places we find ourselves now. The State prevents this dialogue by imposing itself as the constant arbiter between ourselves and our world. The people living on a block can never decide what kind of monument or statue they want to put up on their street. A government planning commission would have to do that. And if you paint a mural on an ugly blank wall the real estate developers left, even if most of your neighbors are delighted by it, the police can take you to jail, and the city will come and paint it over. Paint the mural at night, and they'll start throwing up surveillance cameras all throughout your neighborhood, without asking anyone's permission.

It's no coincidence that a key practice of the global wave of protests these last decades has been taking, holding, and transforming space. Granted, if you're still in open combat with the police, you usually need to keep moving, popping up in one place, disappearing, popping up in another. The State, which

Goodman, August 14, 2017, *Democracy Now!*: www.democracynow.org/2017/8/14/cornel_west_rev_toni_blackmon_clergy (accessed August 19, 2017).

exists by reducing the complexities of the world, has a hard time following us when we take advantage of the strengths of decentralization. A thousand minds thinking and sharing in a web will come up with much more intelligent and creative solutions than a thousand drones following the orders of the institution they work for.

But once we've exhausted them by swarming and dispersing, attacking again and again, we can start to hold space, and the spaces we hold, we can transform. And once we have experience transforming spaces, we begin to realize something about memory: *there is no way all the memory of our oppressions, our dispossessions, our diasporas, our resistance, our mistakes, our betrayals, our complicities, our struggles, our passions, our dreams, and our relations can live inside one person's head, or even a thousand people's heads. We need to engrave our memories in the world around us.*

After Minneapolis police murdered George Floyd, seizing and transforming space became a central practice of the next wave of revolt that erupted and spread around the country and across borders. In the George Floyd rebellion, much of the attention was placed on the burning of the Third Precinct police station, which makes sense. If you can't defeat the police—and this includes torching their vehicles and their logistical centers—you will have little opportunity to turn the world into a healthier place.

But there is another kind of transformation that receives less attention, though it is irreplaceable: the liberation of spaces for memory and healing. This is the battle we fight when the realization dawns on us: if we walk away, what happened will literally just be erased.

In May 2020, my partner Raechel was living on the South Side in Minneapolis, eight blocks from where the cops murdered George Floyd, and she was present throughout the uprising that followed. I wanted to hear more about George Floyd Square, the spot where he died that neighbors took over and transformed. She put me in touch with Arianna Nason, an Anishinaabe from the Fond du Lac Band of Lake Superior Chippewa. "But I'm also a South Sider through and through and I will always call 38th and Chicago home."

On the phone, Arianna tells me:

To understand how it started, you have to step back to a larger scale, and you have to understand what came before.

38th and Chicago has always been a hot block, it's always been spicy out there [*here Arianna gives a laugh; we're talking on the phone but I imagine them throwing their head back a little*]. There's always been some shit going down, always been something shady happening, but there's always been a sense of, *if it's not my business, it's not my business.* As you can imagine, it has been a severely over-policed block for a long time, and people know about that, people talk about that.

It's a Black neighborhood, it's been subjected to redlining, and it's right on the border. If you go a couple blocks in any direction—one block this way, four blocks that way—you come to blocks where historically Black folks were not allowed to buy houses. So you're right on the front line of that violence here. And our neighbors remember what that was like. I don't, because I'm too young, but my auntie next door does.

Next, they tell me the story of Jamar Clark, a Black youth who was murdered by Fourth Precinct cops in North Minneapolis, back in 2015. In response, people occupied all the grounds around the police station:

[...] and we held that down for 18 days. It was from that moment forward that there arose a trend of occupying spaces, at least for this generation of organizers, since that kind of thing has happened before.

Not surprisingly, the government did not indict the officers who had murdered Jamar. And then, when a group of white supremacists went with the express intent of attacking the protest, people expelled them, but one of the racists opened fire on the crowd. Prosecutors gave the racists much lighter charges than they routinely use against us for crimes of resistance in which no person is hurt. Most of them got let off the hook, around the same time it was revealed that they were friends with active-duty cops. Once again, people got an opportunity to see how government is white supremacist to its core:

George Floyd was the absolute final straw for so many people. They immediately took over the Square because there was this habitual pattern that really had started back in 2015. And the way it started was that there were people, neighbors, witnesses, who were on site, knowing that if cops or media got in to "take care of the scene" afterwards, any evidence that was common knowledge, that we had seen, would disappear. So it started with holding the space down, blocking down the area around Cup Foods, immediately shutting down the streets, and people were gathering wherever they could.

So the rebellion actually started with a refusal to let the memory be erased, and a knowledge that that is how the institutions of power would respond:

We started holding community meetings every day at 8am and 7pm, originally out in the open, but then we decided to move it to the Speedway gas station, which totally got looted and destroyed during the first wave of the uprising when people were going through all the commercial stores and taking what they wanted. So we took over the Speedway and called it the People's Way, and it's still called the People's Way because it's painted over the sign. It became a community center. We built a children's play area there, and a library that's still there.

And then there's the People's Closet. That was where we took over some bus shelters and moved them together so people could have a closet, a private space, for our houseless neighbors. See, when the National Guard came, you couldn't be out on the street, so our most vulnerable neighbors, they had nowhere to go, and they were especially exposed to that violence.

There's also the Sanctuary Supply Depot, that's a huge project that's ongoing still, another really good example of an occupied space that got taken over and reclaimed. Eight blocks directly north of the Square, there was a Sheraton Hotel. During the uprising, when a curfew was called, the National Guard was out on the street with an authorization to open fire. If you were on the streets after the curfew, the National Guard could and would shoot you, and they had a mix of live bullets and rubber bullets, so it was a crap shoot. Will they have a metal bullet that will kill you or a so-called less lethal bullet that will leave you permanently disabled?

So people from different groups who had been working with houseless folks, together with some of our most vulnerable neighbors, they took over the Sheraton Hotel and turned it into what they called the Sanctuary. And this was huge. At least half of the Minneapolis population that was experiencing homelessness ended up in that hotel for a while. It was taken over by neighbors, by people who gave a shit. They eventually got kicked out, but they held it down for a couple of months. And then they became known as the Sanctuary Supply Depot, housed out of multiple churches, a bookstore, they bounced around, but they were born directly out of the Sanctuary movement. They became the number one caretaker and the number one supplier of things like tents and warm clothes to the houseless population in Minneapolis.

And the government agencies are not equipped or funded enough to support the houseless population, so they will frequently refer houseless people over to the Sanctuary Depot. And that group is not well funded, they're completely run by mutual aid, completely run by volunteers.

The government, though, pretending like they're there to give support. Yesterday there was a sweep of another camp, everything got bulldozed, everything got destroyed, and the Sanctuary Depot handed out like 35 tents. The city of Minneapolis continues to ignore the most vulnerable population and they continue to displace the homeless. I lost count after 60 sweeps of homeless camps, and that's just from March to December. And meanwhile only one bed is available in the shelters in the whole state.

How are they trying to pacify the movement?

By offering grants, sending in money. Then there's these "community safety initiatives" but they're just rent-a-cops. They just bring in people who have been handpicked by the mayor's office to be their cronies on the streets [...] And the city really likes to use brute force, in and of itself, and that really fucks with us, it really fucks with our morale.

We had these guard shacks on the four intersections that lead into the Square. One is right outside my house. The city threatened a couple times to come and take them away, but each time we showed up in enough force and made them go away. Then they came at like 5:30 in the morning and just took them. That really shook my sense of safety in my own home and my own neighborhood. I had finished painting a mural on the one shack the night before. And the mural just said "people over property always."

That would be the motto of the Square. It's always people over property. We can replace property, we cannot replace life.

All day every day there are still people in the Square holding it down and there are still community meetings and events, family dinners, political education, a couple of us come together for Star Wars night. The People's Way is still there, that's still the main touch point for folks. It's still a functional outdoor community center with a big calendar of events, birthdays, important activities, anniversaries.

There's so many times where I'm having a hard day, feeling a lot of grief, and someone will always be out there.

Throughout my whole writing process, even when this book was just a need bouncing between my heart and my head, I've wanted to explore the relationship between white supremacy or colonial capitalism, and the erasure of memory. I ask Arianna for their view:

White supremacy at its core is isolation. It's alienation and isolation. It alienates us from embodied memory, and it isolates us from our memory, turning it into moments of trauma to be dealt with and not moments of grief to be lived with. White supremacy wants us to forget, whether that be forgetting ourselves, forgetting memory. It wants us to be alone.

Destroying the popular capacity for collectivizing memory, for storytelling, is a necessary strategic task for any oppressive system to be able to reproduce itself. To create dependency, the State systematically produces a new relationship to history: an official history that we passively receive from experts, rather than collective experiences we can dialogue with and draw lessons from.

Patriarchy works alongside whiteness in its erasure of our collective memory. From the centuries-old witch hunts to transphobic legislation today, patriarchy has prioritized the extermination of subversive bodies and experiences. Two friends who helped to foment Bash Back!—the queer anarchist network/rallying cry connected to attacks on homophobic churches, attacks against homophobes in the streets, and resistance to the corporate takeover of the Pride movement—came to visit in Catalunya and gave a talk about this subversion. Queer people, they said, are disinclined to believe leftist narratives of progress, of *things getting better*, because queer and gender nonconforming people have already lived through several moments in which we achieved progress, we achieved spaces of safety and acceptance, and had it brutally wrenched away. One of those moments was Berlin in the 1920s. Another was San Francisco in the '70s. What destroyed those utopias the one time was fascists, and the next time, a homophobic public health policy that enabled the AIDS epidemic to run rampant. Each time, innumerable loved ones were lost and the very memory of queer communities existing defiantly, beautifully, in the open, was erased. And each time, Right and Left collaborated to reinforce a heteronormative and cis culture.

The lesson from this experience is to never trust progress, a new law, coexistence within a tolerant bubble of patriarchal society, or any moral arc imputed to the universe itself. The lesson is that survival is always something to be fought for. Anyone who will not or cannot fulfill the poisonous roles assigned by patriarchy needs to be able to bash back.

Speaking of Bash Back!, they held a convergence in Chicago in the fall of 2023, celebrating the roughly fifteenth anniversary of the group's beginnings. In true form, they continued with their tradition of transforming any space they found themselves in, for example when "a hundred queer anarchist criminals turned a golf course into a public sex forest," according to an anonymous communiqué that goes on to describe how:

We perverted Chicago's Marovitz golf course, had a great night doing it. Imagine the next day, a confounded golfer cautiously lifting a damp towel between two fingers, realizing all at once, their eyes passing over the sex litter drying on the sunny green.

We did this for ourselves, but also to express solidarity with the intractable freaks who held down the Weelaunee Forest [in Atlanta, Georgia, where the struggle against Cop City is taking place]. Since the very first fiery attacks carried out by queers in defense of that place, we've laughed and cried and raged with our feral siblings. If we only defend, we end up with our backs against the wall. All it takes is some boltcutters, encrypted messaging, and trusted friends to open up new fronts in the war for the wild. No more empty rhetoric around "territorial struggle" without a total re-imagining of the terrain. We carved the chaos star into the sand bunker to remind that the forest is a propulsive utopia, spreading in all directions!

In the course of the same convergence, people took over a part of the shore of Lake Michigan and opened it up to nude bathing for all the bodies excluded, stigmatized, and brutally erased in the everyday of capitalist and patriarchal normalcy. Essential to their ability to liberate and transform the park was their ability to kick out the transphobic, homophobic men who tried harassing and filming them, and then to kick out the cops who tried to carry out an arrest in the aftermath.

And, bringing it back to memory, to that fold where the past and the future become indistinguishable, the names of all the comrades and loved ones that folks there had lost since Bash Back! started were shared and remembered in a permanent memorial. Remembering those we've lost and also celebrating our triumphs is a vital part of this fight. That includes those that occurred before we were even born, as well as the ones we got to play a hand in.

I've spent a large part of my life in Catalunya. While living in Barcelona, I put together an anarchist history tour. The walking history tour was already a part of the movement repertoire for holding onto *la memòria històrica*. Historical memory is the kind of memory passed down in stories that transcend the experiences of a single individual, and it's the kind of history that is embodied in relations and communities rather than preserved in archives and museums. Most history tours would focus on a specific time period. I found it really helpful, on the contrary, to mix up stories from all the ages, to show how so much has changed, and at the same time, so little. Weird, magical little patterns emerge, with similar episodes occurring on the same street corners, generation after generation.

One of the people who inspired me to start designing and giving my own history tours, first just to visiting friends, and then more extensively, was Ricard de Vargas. He was giving one of his own history tours when I met him. Ricard went to prison for his participation in armed anticapitalist groups at the end of the Franco dictatorship in Spain. When he got out, the socialists had already shaken hands with the fascists to transition smoothly to democracy without allowing any fundamental social changes to take place. And the million people killed in the Spanish Civil War, all the people jailed, tortured, and killed in the dictatorship: forgotten. Ricard became a movement historian, to fight for the survival of our collective memory.

I remember the feeling of magic on that tour, when Ricard, with the help of some other comrades with a ladder, put a plaque on a wall to mark the spot where an anarchist had fallen decades earlier. No government permission, no grant or official recognition from a historical society: a direct action to reach out and change the world we are forced to live in, to carve a memory on the walls of our city.

Sometimes, governments will put up official monuments to our struggles and plaques for our dead. Sometimes, instead of a violent eviction, they will turn our liberated spaces into a legal park. A few people will have their faith restored in the slow process of petitions and reform. But when that happens, we don't learn how to come together across the divisions they create, we don't learn how to take over the streets, we don't learn how to build power and enact change ourselves. A cracked and orphaned plinth to a statue that is no more tells a story about an ongoing battle for history. A plaque the government may put up to placate us erases this conflict just as it erases our direct role in restoring memory.

The very architecture of this world is a silent monument to their victories against us, a celebration of our deaths and our subjugation. We can topple their most egregious monuments and symbolically this will speak volumes. We can even erect memorials of our own. But placing monuments to people like Frederick Douglass and Emma Goldman within this society that they fought against, and then going no further, would be the greatest erasure of their memory.

We need to remember that it's not just the statue of the slave trader, it's the bank that made its fortunes in slavery and that nowadays makes even more money from sweatshops, mines, and fully automated car factories. The real monuments to that wealth are the skyscrapers and the mansions, the depressing suburbs—wealth in miniature—where the alienated technocrats live. It's the mountaintop removal and gas pipelines, and now industrial-scale solar and wind farms, or the cobalt and lithium mines hiding behind the wholesome branding of the electric cars. It's the redlining, the defunded neighborhoods denied loans, denied clean water or access to fresh food, and it's the police who occupy those neighborhoods. It's the borders, it's the missile factories, it's the surveillance satellites, it's the wars. Because capitalism can only exist where there is artificial scarcity. Because capitalism can only exist on occupied land. Because capitalism can only be implanted among people who have been conquered and colonized.

The Tipping Point

We can push back against the State every day. Sometimes, we succeed in breaking down state control in a collective, visible way. We might even take the struggle farther than it has gone in an entire generation. But our rebellions do not continue indefinitely. Each time, in every place, there is a tipping point—which is often hard to identify until it has already passed—when the forces of order are back in charge and the promise of real change has expired. Since we rarely identify the tipping point in the moment, it is vital for us to understand the wide range of methods the State will use to keep from being overthrown. Quite literally, their tactics range from murdering us to instituting sweeping reforms that *feel* like major victories.

Speaking of the changing strategies the police used to try to impose control after they murdered Mike Brown in August, 2014, Kat from St. Louis tells us:

Mike Brown's body was left, desecrated, in the street for hours, allowing people in the neighborhood to gather, for word to spread, and for confrontation and tensions to immediately grow. Police responded with force— an armored riot vehicle, a helicopter, dogs and assault rifles. As anger on the streets grew, the police were forced to retreat from the scene. The night after the murder there was a vigil that turned into a march and then into the first night of riots, with people leaving the vigil and turning their anger and rage toward the police amassed nearby.

For the next several nights, there are varying levels of demos and street fighting, to which the police respond with a heavy hand. By the fifth night, the governor of Missouri pulled the county police and placed power over the situation in the hands of the state police, which was headed by Ron Johnson, a Black officer. It was like a department level use of "good cop, bad cop," with the state forces promising a gentler hand. The first night that state forces were in control, Ron Johnson walked through the protests and festive resistance, shaking hands and promising a return to order. Despite this, when cruisers tried to enter the area, they were surrounded and chased out, sometimes with broken windows. At the end of the week, footage was released of the alleged theft by Mike Brown from a convenience store, as though this vindicated the cops. The festive mood shifted back into fierce confrontation and renewed looting and rioting. A curfew was put in place by the state but people broke it for several nights, continually pushing at the police lines, throwing Molotov cocktails. There was extreme force used by the state, the National Guard was brought in, and eventually, after a week and half, the police and their political counterparts succeeded in imposing order on W. Florissant.

Very early on, the narrative of the outside agitator that has origins in the civil rights movement across the American South resurfaced. The first time it's heard in the media is from Tom Jackson, the chief of police in Ferguson, that those causing trouble were from the outside. This narrative filters throughout the crowd night after night in visible contradiction to who was actually out in the streets but played on underlying racial tensions. This sentiment really had legs, surfacing again and again in meetings and in the streets, that those causing destruction are from the outside. It disrupts even the most radical of anarchist circles, as tensions around "listening to Black people" manifested into listening to formalized forces of Black power—clergy, churches, local politicians—the "legitimate" voices. Ultimately, people had to make choices about who they wanted to be aligned with. And I will always want to be aligned with the illegitimate voices, those who want to push struggle as far as it can go against power.

There's a lot of outside—concentric circles of power that radiate outward—the family, the neighborhood, the city of Ferguson, the county of St Louis, and so on. There were a lot of attempts to leverage and coopt Mike Brown's family into pacifying the uprising, to varying degrees of success, which eventually fell apart when Darren Wilson wasn't indicted, and Mike Brown's stepfather was outside the Ferguson police department before the public announcement of non-indictment, screaming "burn it all down." The system predictably failed the family.

Quoting again from *Unfinished Acts*, the anonymous publication from the Bay Area:

Even when it is people of color, women, or queer/LGBT people leading campaigns to improve the lives of marginalized groups, they can do little to quell the ongoing deportations, incarcerations, police shootings, poverty, and a million other miseries that remain at an all time high. In Oakland and other progressive regions, we are reminded of the leaders in decolonized countries who replaced colonial elites only to sell out their own people to the IMF and World Bank.

This is how we can understand the two most recent mayors of Oakland whose combined terms in office have pitted them both against the wave of uprisings in this city that began with the January 7 riots and continued into this year with Occupy Oakland. On one hand we have Ron Dellums who came from a prominent family of Black labor leaders in Oakland. He worked as a civil rights activist during the 1960s and would eventually serve as a progressive congressmen and lobbyist before becoming mayor of Oakland. And on the other hand we have Jean Quan who fought for the creation of an Ethnic Studies program at UC Berkeley in 1969 and would follow Dellums as mayor starting in 2011. Both of these civic leaders are well versed in the language of social justice, diversity and civil rights and they both speak as activists and members of social movements. [...]

Although they are well funded, nonprofits such as Youth Uprising did nothing materially to support young people that were arrested in the rebellions, and instead used their resources to make public and paternalistic denunciations of youth who chose to take to the streets. As people of color, many nonprofit leaders used their credibility in communities of color to sell police and media instigated rumors demonizing 'white anarchist outside agitators' as responsible for the riots. By following this narrative, in one move they stripped rebellious youth of their agency and ignored the existence of non-white anarchists and militants.

Idris Robinson, speaking on "strategic potentialities unleashed by the George Floyd rebellion," articulates ten theses that speak to the experiences of the rebellion, drawing on a theoretical legacy and memory of struggle going back generations. In the fifth thesis, he argues:

The so-called "Black leadership," therefore, cannot and does not exist. It is a chimera to be found exclusively in the white liberal imagination.

You hear it everywhere. I've heard it from every city, every friend who texted me. If I called a friend and said, "Hey, what happened in NOLA?", or "What happened in Chicago?" If there were riots, if people got busy, there was no mention of a Black leadership. If things stopped, if things were stultified, all we heard about was a Black leadership.

The thing is, I have never in my life actually seen a Black leader. Why? Because they don't exist. If there are Black leaders, they're dead like Martin and Malcolm. If you're worth your salt, you will be killed. If there are Black leaders, they are in jail with Mumia and with Sundiata. If there are Black leaders, they are on the run with Assata.[10]

This is reminiscent of the pattern that helped to destroy the Civil Rights/Black Power Movement of the '60s and '70s. According to Modibo Kadalie:

During our teenage years we had witnessed and participated in the early sit-ins as foot soldiers. We watched the emergence of all manner of opportunist, petit bourgeois leaders with extremely limited goals within the context of their reformist visions and circumscribed agendas [...] all of the self-creativity of the movement was being discredited as mindless "spontaneity" which needed to be organized, directed, and orchestrated. Interestingly, just at the point when these "organizations" were most active, the movement began to seriously stall. It appeared to some of us that the more these "organizations" intervened, the more inert the movement became.[11]

10   Idris Robinson, "how it might should be done," Chicago, IL: Ill Will Editions, 2020, p.11.
11   Modibo Kadalie, "Introduction" in Kimathi Mohammed, *Organization and Spontaneity*, p.12.

There was a similar effect in Oakland in 2009, when the figures of past resistance showed up more as valuable museum pieces in a collection rather than as a living body of experiences that younger folks could draw on. According to *Unfinished Acts*:

> Unfortunately the strong legacy of the Panthers has also had a demobilizing effect in Oakland where many ex-Panthers have joined nonprofits, ran for political office, or started commercial enterprises using their previous revolutionary careers as selling points. Despite their exemplary militancy, the over-fetishization of the Panthers prevents a collective recounting and critique of their shortcomings, such as their authoritarian and hierarchical organizational structure, and prevents the rebels of today from effectively fighting into the future while both learning and breaking from the past.

Lorenzo Kom'boa Ervin, a veteran of the original Black Panther Party, declares: "The Party's over. Build something new!"

> The stage of building revolutionary movements based on the Communist Party vanguard model was proven bankrupt by the mid-1970s, as communist movements fell all over the world. The idea of central leadership and cult of personality fell with it, although the Black movement, especially religious organizations like the Nation of Islam continue with that model.[12]

Widening his critique, Ervin points out how the Black bourgeoisie is an important element in protecting racial capitalism:

---

12 Lorenzo Kom'boa Ervin, *Anarchism and the Black Revolution*, London: PM Press, 2021. All quotes in this paragraph from p.117.

he calls it "the mis-leadership of the Negrosie." Ervin is clear about the need for multiracial solidarity, but without diluting it in a feel-good coalition that ignores real power differences. Instead, he describes a process of building a coalition among "the urban Black poor and their non-white allies." Note the absence of both whites and upper middle-class or wealthy people of any race in this formulation. Later, he mentions that getting support from solidaristic whites is an aspiration, but he phrases this as a need to "split the white working class,"[13] again showing a balance between seeing revolution as necessarily multiracial and also distrusting white people. White people with a sense of history will understand that this distrust is reasonable.

One of the things that reactionary authoritarian groups like the Nation of Islam have in common with progressives who use representational politics for career-building and class-climbing is that both tend to encourage the segregation of the oppressed. The oppressed need to stay in stable, essentialized demographics so that leaders can claim to represent them and speak for them. And, as Frantz Fanon pointed out over half a century ago, speaking from the experience of liberation movements in the colonies, would-be authorities need to demonstrate to the current authorities that they are ready to be given a chance to rule; they do this by showing that they are able to pacify and demobilize the rebellious movements they claim to lead.

Writing on the riots after UK police killed Mark Duggan in 2011, Lorenzo Kom'boa Ervin decries all the white activists who supported the dominant narratives in the media and distanced themselves from the uprising rather than participating in it: "If the so-called Anarchist 'Black Bloc' of white

13   Ervin, *Anarchism*, all quotes in this paragraph from p.121.

youth had joined with inner city Black kids, we may have had a general insurrection of long-standing and major damage to the state and capital."[14]

But instead we get peace police. "Legitimate voices" and the appointed representatives of oppressed communities—those with access to wealth and institutional power—will denounce the uprisings as "looting" and wanton criminality. They will blame the disturbances on outside agitators, depersonalized youth who supposedly can't think for themselves, or dehumanized criminals deserving punishment. The media and politicians posing as sympathetic will amplify these claims. Then, professional activists working for the leaders will instrumentalize white college kids who are looking to show off an antiracist image by engaging in comfortable, low-risk activism, getting them to extend the leaders' power and act as peace police in marches and protests.

The peace police follow a script that actually reinforces white supremacy and puts all of us in danger. They try to isolate anyone in the crowd who starts breaking laws (this may include breaking bank windows, painting messages on the walls, throwing things at police, erecting barricades, or even just walking in the street). They do this to people of any race, exposing them to arrest, and sometimes performing a "citizens' arrest" and handing them over to the police. In the

---

14 Ervin, *Anarchism*, p.167. I also feel the need to point out, after speaking with several people who were in the streets those days, that a number of white anarchists did in fact participate in this uprising. Over all, it was the progressive white Left that spread media narratives denouncing it. Nonetheless, much of the anarchist participation was ineffective or timid, and Ervin's and similar criticisms were part of a vital process of reflection that manifested in antiracist rebellions occurring just a few years later in the UK taking on a much more multiracial character.

process, they prevent the crowd from building the capacity to defend itself or to transform the urban space they are moving through. Secondly, they spread the narrative that white people are to blame for "ruining" or "disrupting" the march by fighting police or vandalizing white supremacist institutions.

The trope of blaming outside agitators came up in the uprisings in Oakland, Tottenham, Ferguson, Portland, Minneapolis, Atlanta—nearly everywhere people took the streets. If a group of people unilaterally push a protest in one direction without any concern for anyone else there, that's a problem, especially if they are white and those most affected by the issue are people of color, or if they are well-to-do and those most affected are poor. If people participate in a struggle, and they don't contribute to supporting the prisoners or the families of those who die or become disabled, that's a problem, especially if they are white or upper class. But most people who weaponize the trope of privileged agitators are usually demonizing the very act of liberating space. By suggesting that fighting back is a privileged act, they are instilling in us the subconscious belief that a capitalist, white supremacist system can be gently pressured into saving us from capitalism and white supremacy.

Are Black and Indigenous people far more affected by police violence than white people? Yes, overwhelmingly so. In a resistance movement, should folks take cues and learn from the experiences of those most affected by the institution or system they are struggling against? Again, yes, without a doubt.

Additionally, pretty much everyone who is not a rich, white, cis-gendered person faces the threat of harm and abuse at the hands of police. Some people, like those experiencing a mental health crisis in public (that is, those not rich enough to be able to have their breakdowns at a resort) and trans people, are even more disproportionately likely to die at the hands of police. Furthermore, we are harmed when those we care about are harmed.

Let's not forget Rayshard Brooks, who was shot in the back and killed by Atlanta cops in a Wendy's parking lot on June 12, 2020. Rayshard was a young Black man out on probation from a prison sentence. When the police killed him, people revolted. They were already enraged with the police, and in the spirit of the ongoing George Floyd Rebellion, they torched the Wendy's and turned the area into a liberated zone and a memorial for nearly a month.

Despite the popularity of the revolt, peace police started circulating the rumor that the *person* (it was actually a crowd) who trashed and torched the Wendy's was *a white person*, therefore, a privileged person not actually harmed by the police, therefore, not a valid participant in the riot, therefore, *an outside agitator*. An ambiguous title that means: *maybe even a cop!* The sordid possibility that the cops had engineered the riot sent hundreds of (mostly white) internet sleuths into paroxysms of excitement. They got to work poring over all the footage they could find.

That many people are ignorant about what a revolt entails, and what kinds of police tactics we need to protect ourselves from, presents us with another huge problem. People are more likely to be carrying phones and cameras in hand at a riot, rather than much more useful things like a hammer, a can of spray paint, a gas can, a first aid kit, a water bottle, extra masks, bottle rockets, a lighter, or a sound system.

Soon enough, the sleuths had a clear image of her face, and then her identity: Natalie White. She was arrested and charged with arson. Turns out, she was Rayshard Brooks' girlfriend. She was hauled in and sent to trial along with two Black men.

Then there was the case of the white online activist who was spreading conspiracy theories that a Black man who set fire to the abandoned police precinct in Seattle was actually a provocateur working for the cops. Coincidentally, also on June 12, 2020, Kristina Beverlin shared several photos she had taken of him near the self-declared Capitol Hill Autonomous Zone and tweeted "I need everyone in Seattle to retweet the photo of this man […] there is NO WAY he was acting alone." Within a few days, thanks to her citizen sleuthing, he was identified. And since, predictably, he was not a cop and not part of any conspiracy, he got locked up. I contacted Beverlin to communicate that at a minimum, she should support the defense fund of the person whose life she was actively ruining. Not surprisingly, she refused. White supremacists who act like part of the movement and may even think they are, are often the most dangerous. Photographing resistance actions and spreading conspiracy theories, they put us directly at risk. Meanwhile, neighborhoods like Capitol Hill face an increase in racist police violence as entitled, economically advantaged people like Beverlin flood in. Attacking the police is not a provocation or a conspiracy, it is a reasonable response to situations like this.

These various forms of sowing conflict and infighting don't always stop us, but they do harm our movements, and they lead to collective exhaustion. The arrests, the beatings, the conflicts glossed over or unresolved, the presence of patriarchal, ableist, and racist dynamics throughout our society, and the urgent need to organize jail and legal support ... when we go up against a society this damaging, this pervasive, the list of things that can exhaust us or crush us is unending.

The truth is, very few rebellions grow in a linear fashion, getting bigger and bigger until we overthrow the State and have a chance to make something new. One thing we forget is to not hang all our hopes on an exponential growth of revolt; we forget about the other forms of transformation and creation we need to push forward in the space of the revolt. At some point in our revolts, things will start to cool down, and that is when the progressive politicians step back in to propose the next wave of reforms.

Today, such a short time after all those fires were lit, many people have forgotten that the only impetus for change came from our *illegal* anti-police and antiracist rebellions. Now most police across the US have to wear body cameras to check if they are actually committing misdeeds, and these are increasingly being used in the UK as well, though it's no surprise police began systematically misusing them almost immediately.[15] For basically the first time in US history, police are occasionally going to prison for murdering poor people and racialized people. None of these reforms have stopped police racism and brutality. If anything, police have pushed back against all the protests by accelerating the rate at which they murder people, in their daily duties and also in situations of protest.[16] At the beginning of 2023, they executed the anar-

---

15 National Policing Institute, "Police Body Cameras: What Have We Learned Over Ten Years of Deployment?" June 2020. Bill Hutchinson, "Recent high-profile deaths put police body cameras under new scrutiny", *ABC News*, 5 March 2023. Noel Titheradge, "Police officers widely misusing body-worn cameras," *BBC*, 27 September 2023.

16 According to "Mapping Police Violence," https://mapping policeviolence.us/ (accessed March 9, 2024), police killings have increased over the last ten years. The vast majority (98.1 percent) of police who kill someone are not even charged with a crime, and of the few who are charged, only about one in four are convicted. Earlier data is harder to come by since most police forces do not release statistics, but all other sources consulted suggest an increase going back to 2010 or earlier, for example, the Law Enforcement

chist land defender Tortuguita (Manuel Esteban Pael Terán), who was participating in the Stop Cop City protest in the Weelaunee Forest in Atlanta. In 2020, they executed the anti-fascist Michael Reinoehl who had shot a neo-fascist who was engaged in a coordinated assault on protesters in Portland. The year before that, they executed the anarchist Willem van Spronsen who was setting fire to vehicles at an immigration prison in Tacoma, Washington. And over 2016 and 2017, they permanently injured and almost killed multiple people trying to stop the Dakota Access Pipeline. Over the same years, they have frequently associated with white supremacist groups or stood by as white supremacists drove their cars through protests, killing or seriously injuring dozens of people. And several friends of Mike Brown, murdered by police in Ferguson in 2014, turned up dead in suspicious circumstances after the rebellion, leading surviving friends and neighbors to accuse the police of carrying out extrajudicial executions.

Greece and Chile were the sites of two of the most powerful uprisings in the last two decades. After massive police interventions failed to suppress those uprisings and the government decided not to send in the military because of the risk of losing control completely, the Left swept into power in both countries. And in both countries, the Left introduced groundbreaking referendums that would have upended historical power dynamics in an almost revolutionary way. In Greece,

Epidemiology Project at the University of Illinois Chicago: https://policeepi.uic.edu/data-civilian-injuries-law-enforcement/facts-figures-injuries-caused-law-enforcement/ (accessed April 20, 2024). Prior to 2009, there are extremely few documented cases of police being charged with murder, first- or second-degree homicide. In the vast majority of killings, no charges are brought, and in the few cases of charges and convictions, they are lesser charges with short or no jail sentences.

the referendum won in an overwhelming popular vote. The government refused to implement it. As Tasos Sagris puts it:

The people felt abandoned and betrayed by the social democrats and so they went to Syriza [the coalition party of the Left]. And Syriza, instead of educating them in anticapitalism and supporting the social struggles, they decided to abandon even the leftist tradition and go back to the social democratic center. So the people felt betrayed for a second time, in five years, from 2010 to 2015 they were betrayed twice.

In Chile, the referendum effort fell apart due to squabbling and infighting, though the Left managed to hold on to power. In both countries, placing hope in the democratic process took people off the streets and gave the State the chance to reconstitute its power.

This was not a coincidence, and it was entirely predictable (in fact, anarchists in both countries and around the world predicted exactly what ended up happening). If the State cannot defeat us one way, they will try to defeat us another.

Black anarchist William C. Anderson talks about how reformism is especially harmful to Black communities and anyone else who faces conditions that threaten their survival:

As we deteriorate, advocates of an incremental approach to deadly situations put lives at risk whether they mean to or not. They insist that the intolerable be tolerated for some unspecified but never-ending period of time. Over and over, problems too big to be reformed away are given new chances to be rewired—and we're somehow shocked every time things remain the same […] So while we wait ad infinitum for reforms to chip away at what's enchaining us, more and more lives are lost, just to give the reformers the opportunity to specify again what is not working. This is unequivocally true across the board for reforms in the areas of "criminal justice," economics, and civil rights. Black people know these reform strug-gles all too well.[17]

The State has developed the counterinsurgency playbook internationally, going back more than half a century: in Algiers, Detroit, Pine Ridge, and Los Angeles; in Kenya, Vietnam, Italy, Spain, Chile, and Israel; and more recently in Argen-tina, Iraq, México, and Greece. The balance of brutality and bribery always depends on questions of race, class, indigeneity, and country status, but the methodology is the same. And we can see the final chapter of the playbook at work right now, in Santiago and Athens, in Istanbul, Hong Kong, Bristol, and Oakland. Once they have exhausted us, traumatized us, split us, imprisoned us, killed us, or bought us off, they come back in, reimpose order, and—most importantly—they rewrite what happened so that we will never learn our lessons.

17   William C. Anderson, *The Nation on No Map*, Oakland, CA: AK Press, 2021, p.6.

CHAPTER 2

They Will Sell Us Memories That Are Not Our Own

What would have happened if the conquerors had been defeated? If the monarchs and private companies of Western Europe had failed in their invasion of Turtle Island? If the peoples of West Africa had been able to burn the slave forts and stop the most brutal wave of enslavement in human history?

What would that have even looked like?

It's not just wishful thinking. All the ingredients for decisively defeating colonialism and the emergence of the modern State were present in the fifteenth, sixteenth, and seventeenth centuries. We have examples of horizontal Indigenous societies defeating much better equipped European powers; peoples targeted by invasion or enslavement discouraging collaboration with the colonizers and spreading a shared anticolonial consciousness over a huge area; revolutionary movements holding out for decades in Europe itself, undermining the power of the conquerors on their home turf.

Rather than being defeated and turning to pacifism, it would not have been so impossible for Anabaptist revolutionaries to have maintained their hold on a few central European cities in the 1400s and 1500s. After all, central state control was still patchy in Europe at this time, and in the actual history they demonstrated a use of new technologies and tactics capable of defeating the aristocratic cavalries that had previously dominated battlefields. Such a victory would have helped—and required—them to learn the lesson that political centrism and the creation of new states wouldn't give them any advantages; it would only ensure betrayal.

Meanwhile, by the late 1500s, Spanish, Portuguese, and English invaders were experiencing their first major defeats in Abya Yala or Turtle Island (the continent the invaders christened the Americas, and which they considered to be two continents). By that time, the Indigenous peoples had ample opportunity to see that the most powerful states fell the quickest to the colonizers, and the remaining state mechanisms were easily repurposed by the victors to accelerate colonization and enslavement. In the actual history, there was a great deal of solidarity across peoples and a culture opposing collaboration with the colonizers. A prime example is the anticolonial confederation built up by Tecumseh and Tenskwatawa. Emphasizing that culture and achieving more solidaristic alliances across regions would have changed the strategic landscape significantly.

At the same time, Indigenous peoples in the Americas were gaining new allies: people from West Africa who had been captured by local states, sold to European slave traders, and shipped to brutal plantations and mines on the other side of the Atlantic. The maroons were those who successfully rebelled and escaped, fleeing into the mountains and swamps in territories that would be given the names Brazil, Suriname, Jamaica, Haiti, Florida, Carolina ... Across the board, they acted in solidarity with or absorbed into local Indigenous societies and won a significant number of defensive wars against modern states.

Back in West Africa, where the most powerful local states were profiting off the slave trade to expand their power, there were entire regions that were off-limits to slave traders due to effective local resistance. For the first centuries of that geno-cidal trade, peoples like the Jola, Dagomba, Malinke, and Balanta protected their territory, won wars against empires, and made alliances and peace treaties with the purpose of stopping or limiting slave raiding. Transatlantic enslavement accelerated greatly in the 1600s, causing more displacement and wars in West Africa. The slave-trading empires certainly didn't win every battle, and they didn't even win every war. One or two of them collapsing could have encouraged the local anti-slavery alliances to become even more powerful.

Also in the late 1600s, there were multiple instances of solidarity between Anabaptists or other heretical Christians and local Indigenous peoples, particularly in the areas renamed New England and New Netherlands. Rather than an uncomfortable position between religious refugees and non-consensual settlers, if they had been empowered by more victories and a stronger practice of solidarity back in Europe, the Anabaptists and their native neighbors might have won a small revolution against the genocidal Puritans. This also would have created liberated port towns with European intermediaries who could have helped local peoples acquire European guns without acquiescing to the disempowering trades that the colonizers imposed.

In the same decades, many of the poorest Europeans—and also a number of Africans—forced to work in the transatlantic ships were carrying out successful mutinies and turning to piracy. With more defeats in their invasion of Turtle Island, Indigenous peoples better equipped to resist them, a harder time enslaving people in Africa and thus a strict limitation to the plantation system that fueled the economic motor of colonial expansion, and with resurgent revolutionary movements in their home countries—not to mention an Atlantic Ocean and Caribbean Sea increasingly unsafe for merchants as piracy gained a better foothold—the modernizing European states could easily have collapsed.

No new technology, belief system, or anachronistic knowledge of the future would have been required to prevent the world of extreme crisis we live in now. Better luck, better strategic decisions in a few cases, and a better job of learning the lessons of prior generations could have crashed the emerging world system. The United States would never have been born. The main architects of colonialism would have been overthrown, as so many states throughout history have been. The current nightmare of global capitalism we are currently inhabiting would not have been born.

This alternate world would not be perfect. The struggle would not be over. Several states would probably still exist throughout the world, trying to impose their empires, trying to conquer their neighbors and enslave their own subjects. But the globalization of a particularly dangerous military and economic model would have been defeated. And in our actual history, it was that exponential acceleration in the techniques of extraction and domination—that influx in power and resources—that allowed the modern state to form and capitalism to control the destiny of the entire planet. In this alternate reality, the strongest global networks would actually belong to the liberated territories, to the peoples who successfully fended off invasions or overthrow their states.

As we open our eyes to the real twenty-first century and the apocalypse we're currently facing, what is one of the most illuminating differences that alternate reality presents? No ecocide on a global scale. No climate crisis. No mass extinction event. No millions of climate refugees. No loss of food security or clean water experienced by the majority of the world's population.

In parallel, for all the countless researchers, theorists, and outright hacks who are paid to uphold faith in capitalism, I have not come across a single one who has made a well researched argument that capitalism could have developed globally without causing all the ecological devastation we now take for granted. Few people even *try* to make that argument.

So if the current ecological crisis is so inextricably wrapped up with our unfolding history of colonialism and state power, why doesn't the topic of undoing colonialism ever come up in polite conversation? Of actually abolishing the United States, and Canada, and Brazil, and Chile, and México, and all the European powers that founded them? How are we supposed to grant any credibility to the absurd idea that ending fossil fuel use without abolishing banks is going to save us?

Likewise, why do most people think of something completely different when "environmentalism" gets brought up? Why are they not thinking about Lef-Traru, Nanny of the Maroons, Guaitipan, Tȟašúnke Witkó, Wat Tyler, or Gerrard Winstanley if you ask them to think about environmentalists of the past?

Why, in fact, are so many of us never even told of these resistance movements? Do they truly lack relevance? Maybe the reason is that, if we realized their relevance and their continuing resonance today, we might pose a real danger to the existing social order, to the institutions that control our education and our sense of history.

The Hammer

The meaning of environmentalism—the idea of defending the land, protecting our ecology—has not always been as superficial as mainstream discourse would have us believe.

More accurately, there has always been an intense battle waged for the heart of what we even mean by concepts like "the land" and "nature." We learn the surprising fact in *Whigs and Hunters*, by E.P. Thompson, that at the birth of the modern era in the United Kingdom, you could be put to death for hiding your identity by wearing a mask or blackening your face with charcoal. The reason is because the lower classes had long ago been robbed and displaced, and farming was no longer carried out in a communal manner to feed communities. It was carried out on plantations to grow cash crops, enrich plantation owners, and keep the workers alive with a minimal, unhealthy diet. However, thanks to their struggles, they had held onto other commons, like wells and rivers for drinking water, reeds, rushes, and fishing; pastures for grazing herd animals they relied on for milk or wool; and forests for wood (their main fuel source), medicinal herbs (an important resource for healing), and hunting (the only way for many poorer people to get meat, as well as a necessary form of participation in local ecosystems to balance the populations of larger herbivores).[18]

For centuries, an intense class conflict was waged over access to the forests, with aristocrats preferring the notion of "private property," so they could reserve forests for sport hunting. However, the war to defend the commons was lost when large, straight-trunked trees became increasingly rare, at the same time as they became an increasingly strategic resource for

---

18 Humans have been an essential predator and vital part of nearly every land and coastal ecosystem on the planet for tens of thousands or hundreds of thousands of years, depending on the continent. For a more thorough rebuttal to the colonial idea that "humans cause" the climate crisis or the ecological crisis, see Peter Gelderloos, *The Solutions Are Already Here: Strategies for Ecological Revolution from Below.*

state power. Oceangoing ships transported enslaved people and plundered resources, and they were the backbone of an effective, global military. The Spanish crown had not taken good enough care of its forests. Swathes of the Iberian peninsula are still desertified today due in part to Spain's naval extractivism, and when those forests were lost, it meant the crown would have to import lumber to rebuild its fleets.

The British Parliament would not be so shortsighted. They would become "environmentalists," and all the remaining forests would become private property or state property, no matter how many thousands of peasants they needed to murder. Because when commoners went into the forests for firewood, they didn't chop down entire trees. They had long since developed a sustainable practice of taking dead wood and cutting branches off living trees. Their clippings wouldn't kill the trees. But it would prevent them from growing straight trunks, making the trees useless as masts on transatlantic schooners. And when the commoners started blackening their faces to preserve their anonymity while illegally hunting, gathering, or collecting wood, the government decided that trespassing or hiding one's identity should be punishable by death.

Here we have two diametrically opposed paradigms of environmentalism or land defense. In the one, humans are separate from nature, humans are the threat to nature, and parks of strategic natural resources need to be demarcated and protected—by government force—from human incursion. However, nature is a suitable zone for humans to enter temporarily, for entertainment purposes like sport hunting.

In the other, humans are a part of nature, we are ecological beings, we relate to an ecosystem through traditional practices that are respectful, sustainable, and that guarantee our collective survival and fulfillment. Nature is a commons. Different cultures give a different emphasis on whether it belongs to us or we belong to it. Regardless, the relationship is inalienable. And the major threat to nature, to the commons, and to all life, is the State: that massive conglomeration of institutions that pursues its expansionist interests by organizing commerce, extraction, military conquest, and whatever religion it finds most effective for justifying the order of things.

This dichotomy, and the brutality with which the aristocrats inflict their version of environmentalism, becomes even more extreme in the colonies, where environmentalism is still used today as an excuse to police, displace, and kill Indigenous peoples.

Nonetheless, ecology from below has never been fully erased, not even in the countries that led the wars against the commons.

Anna is a researcher and movement participant who has lived for many years in the UK. She shares some of the history, forgotten or invisible, that provides part of the foundation for the movement today:

Anti-road campaigning of the '90s gave birth to the ecological direct action movement in the UK. Many people started to feel empowered and joined EarthFirst!, a broadly green anarchist direct action movement, or banner, that sought to challenge ecologically destructive industrial developments and defend the wild. But from its beginning in the UK, it had a much deeper and more intersectional analysis of what drives ecological and social degradation, the relationship to class, state power, colonialism, heteronormativity, and so on. People spent years debating these things, writing, exploring. (See *Do or Die*, for instance, which came out of Brighton in the '90s). And they practiced solidarity, through links with the Sarawak and Canada, among others, by visiting and supporting communities inside and outside Europe. A good example is the long campaign to stop industrial development in Iceland that loads of people from the UK were involved in.

But they also pointed to class dimensions (think blood sport/hunting by aristocrats) and other social and racial inequalities. Many had and have developed eco-anarchist analyses and understandings and strategies.

Since then, there have been plenty of movements, groups, and campaigns that have been more radical in their political analyses and tactics than contemporary "environmentalist" movements—[here, Anna pauses in the interview to interject "how much I hate that word!"]—that created spaces of resistance and cultures of resistance, spaces that were anticapitalist, anti-state, antiracist, queer, abolitionist. They explicitly targeted the corporations responsible for ecological destruction, the state actors, the networks of power and profitability, they called out the (neo)colonial entanglements, and the outsourcing of destruction, whether in the form of mining, waste, or other.

And they created spaces of care and solidarity, built relationships and connections.

The British state responded with intense repression, though following a policing model that largely operated from the shadows:

The state claims to be doing something they call "consensual policing", but a closer look at policing in practice reveals that this was only ever a myth. British policing, and repression more widely, are based on intense surveillance, control, and coercion. In the past few decades, repression had devastating effects on movements, especially through the combination of precarity, austerity, repression, and undercover infiltration.

The latter is of course not unique to the UK, but I'm not aware of any country that employed and allowed similar levels of deception, state violence, and cover-ups in relation to the employment of undercover cops to infiltrate and destroy movements. They were in romantic relationships with women that were active in these movements for years, fathered children, abused trust, and caused incredible amounts of harm and pain.

One of the worst effects of this type of repression was the breakdown of trust, the active spread of mistrust within movements, which really weakened radical groups and of course their organizing and the actions people undertook. And yes, it led to the loss of collective memories, older generations dropped out, or focused on seeking justice for those who were affected the worst by undercover infiltration. Others just left organizing altogether.

What we have to realize, when it comes to repression, is that this is not a reactive process on the part of the State. The State does not passively respond to crime. It has always organized repression as an offensive measure against the societies it governs, to divide, to surveil, to intimidate, and to eliminate. The process of repression begins with the State proactively defining crime so as to prepare the battlefield to its advantage.

Thus, theft means stealing food from a convenience store or stealing a tourist's iPhone; it does not mean reducing our wages, inflating our rent, plundering the wealth of an entire society, or taking away a community's food source. Murder means shooting a single person, in an environment in which you have been humiliated your entire life, in which a capitalist, racist, patriarchal culture sells you harmful models for how to earn respect. It does not mean sending military aid to Israel so that another 30,000 Palestinians are killed, or making $12 billion in revenue manufacturing PFAS and other carcinogens, increasing by half our chances of heart attack and doubling the chances that we'll get a lethal form of cancer.[19]

If you doubt that the criminal justice system is part of a war that the State systematically wages against its population—the social war—consider the following. Governments will intentionally change their laws to pacify our movements, turning something legal into a crime. When the UK campaign to Stop Huntington Animal Cruelty (SHAC) almost bankrupted a major killer of animals—the Huntington vivisection company—through an effective boycott campaign that also targeted companies that did business with them, the UK government simply made organizing effective boycotts a crime and put SHAC organizers in prison for several years.

Conspiracy laws have a similar history, as do laws against wearing masks and concealing our identity.

---

19 In just the first four months of the latest genocidal campaign, Israel killed approximately 30,000 Palestinians, the vast majority non-combatants, and forced 2 million out of their homes while subjecting them to conditions of starvation and epidemics. The approximate 2023 revenue of DuPont, one of the main manufacturers of toxic PFAS "forever chemicals" was $12 billion. On the risk increase associated with PFAS exposure, the research is abundant. For examples, see www.sciencedirect.com/science/article/pii/S0160412023005238 (accessed April 20, 2024) and https://sph.umich.edu/news/2023posts/exposure-to-pfas-chemicals-doubles-the-odds-of-a-prior-cancer-diagnosis-in-women.html (accessed April 20, 2024).

If we find an effective tactic of resistance, they will turn it into a crime.

The anarchist slogan, *if voting changed anything, they would have made it illegal*, comes with a high degree of historical accuracy.

After waves of effective sabotage actions against luxury housing developments, lumber companies, SUV dealerships, and other enterprises engaged in ecocide—actions in which no one was harmed—the US government changed their laws in the '90s and '00s so that people carrying out ecologically motivated sabotage could be charged with terrorism.[20]

In multiple waves of arrests, dozens of people were threatened with spending the rest of their lives in prison, many were pushed into snitching, and some committed suicide. Under pressure, others turned towards upper-class or nationalist versions of environmentalism. Beyond those directly caught up in trials, an entire movement was hammered, as were the friends and families of those who died, went on the run, or were locked away. Tragically, the weaknesses that caused parts of the movement to crack were repeats of mistakes that earlier struggles had already learned from but had few ways to pass on.

Nonetheless, most people learned fast how to stay strong in the face of repression, how to survive prison, how to provide effective trial and prison support. People who were passed through the gears of repression continue to stay radical and strong, people like Marius Mason who is still locked up, and people like Eric McDavid and Daniel McGowan who made it out the other side, as well as all their loved ones. They continue to fight for the earth from a place that is intersec-

20   Will Potter, *Green Is the New Red: An Insider's Account of a Social Movement Under Siege*, San Francisco, CA: City Lights, 2011.

tional and solidaristic. And yet, we would have come out of it so much stronger if we had grown up nourished by the stories of those who had gone through similar waves of repression decades earlier. Most of the people in my circles didn't have any radical elders: we had to learn those stories from books (often distorted by the lenses of academic and authoritarian-leaning historians), or in tiny snippets in letters from long-term prisoners.

In *Green Scared? Some Lessons from the FBI Crackdown on Eco-Activists*, the anarchist publishing collective CrimethInc provides vital analysis of the lessons learned or relearned, but at the time, in the thick of it, it wasn't yet clear what our strengths and weaknesses were against a campaign of targeted repression.

It's still stressful to write about this now, because of the way the government will bring politically motivated charges against their enemies even decades later, and that anxiety and fear is one of the goals of repression:

It was around that time we discovered the FBI were investigating us. A sympathizer with a normal job adjacent to the public bureaucracy informed us that the feds were asking for a couple of us by name. I filed a Freedom of Information Act request for any open investigations that named me. I got a curt response that there were no such investigations, with a footnote that they were allowed to exclude mention of any cases that fell under antiterrorism. We knew there was an investigation, thanks to our good relationships in the community. Their official response meant it was either being kept off the books or they were angling for terrorism charges against at least some of the anarchists in town. Either way it didn't look good.

For a small town in rural Virginia, we were doing a decent job of holding it down. With just about a dozen people, we maintained a weekly Food Not Bombs that was partially led by houseless comrades; we started a Copwatch with a local Black activist to curb police harassment in the neighborhood; we ran an Anarchist Black Cross that supported long-term political prisoners and organized with folks locked up in the Supermax prisons, together with their family members, who were fighting against solitary confinement and other torture methods that were being used against those who resisted.

During those same years, there were a fairly large number of sabotage attacks the police had never been able to solve, against targets connected to ecocide, capitalist alienation, and the US war machine. It would not be out of character for the FBI to put known anarchists in prison for decades, either by threatening prison time to get someone to snitch, or by manufacturing evidence.

I didn't want to go back to prison. So I left town, set up a way for trusted friends to contact me in case it looked like the police were making a move, and started researching what would be required to go underground.

A long time has passed since then. Our movements have gotten better at supporting people on the run, thanks to a combination of learning from past movements and being attentive to current circumstances. One friend living under a false name in a country far from his home helped put together an underground publication, a little book of testimonials written by people living in clandestinity. The book wasn't put on the internet: it was something more real, an artisanal edition passed from person to person, hand bound by people relearning the use of tools that we can make ourselves, rather than the kind of machinery that control those who use it. *Samizdat* was the name for illegal, DIY editions that came out in parts of the Soviet bloc to spread subversive ideas under the noses of the censors, and it is a tradition that has always flaunted borders.

Clandestinity can grind you down. The solitude. The obligation to flee the territory you've been pouring your heart into and risking your life and freedom for.

But with support, with whole communities of struggle phasing in and out of clandestinity, the experience can be completely different. Over a decade ago, a network of Mapuche communities in struggle invited a group of anarchists from other countries to extend their links of international solidarity in new directions.

For much of that first solidarity trip, we were hosted by a family, José Llanquileo, Angélica, and their son. The three of them had lived in clandestinity for three years and Angélica had given birth while they were on the run. They finally got caught when a neighbor decided to snitch for a big pay-out. When we met them, Angélica had gotten out already, and José was nearing the end of his sentence, able to leave during the days for work release.

Angélica described the hardships of clandestinity:

> For one thing, you don't have any peace of mind. On top of that, you can't plan for the future or have any projectuality. While you're eating breakfast, you'll be keeping your eyes on the road outside, ready to run at any time.

One time, a caravan of 400 cops with buses, tanks, water cannons, and jeeps came to arrest them, a huge display of force to show the futility of resistance. But Angélica saw the caravan when it was still on the other side of the lake, and they ran for the hills.

Later on that trip, we were taken to a night-time meeting with a Mapuche *weichafe*, or warrior, who faced 73 years in prison for actions taken for the liberation of Wallmapu, the Mapuche country. He said that usually, the police would catch you within two years of going on the run, but he explained that "going on the run can show contempt for state justice and a refusal to submit to their institutions." And despite all the violence directed against his people by the settler states of Chile and Argentina, and the very personal threat hanging over his head, he was calm. Clearly, he was not isolated; he was still a part of his struggle and of his people, even if he had to move frequently, arrange night-time meetings, and stay away from places he had lived previously. I remember him laughing frequently as he told stories and tried to impart the most vital features of their struggle: "The Mapuche struggle has all it needs. And we're always three steps ahead of the state."

Jameel Winston has been in prison for almost thirty years, since he was a teenager. We first met when he was in a Supermax prison far in the southwestern corner of Virginia (a seven-hour drive from where his family, and most prisoners' families live), and when I was in Harrisonburg helping run the Anarchist Black Cross. Jameel told me how he grew up in a majority Black city in Virginia not knowing anything about the history of Black resistance and revolutionary movements. Through tremendous dedication, he found the resources to educate himself about this history on the inside, but the entire system—inside and out—is designed to keep oppressed people from making this choice and to deny them the connections and relationships that would make it easier. Nonetheless, by the time we started working together, Jameel was an experienced revolutionary and one of the organizers of a series of protests and strikes that were starting to break out. We began doing what we could to support them, to make it easier for family to visit, to let the guards know there would be consequences if they came down too hard on the folks on the inside.

Despite all the retaliation, Jameel told me that has been one of the high points of his time on the inside, because resistance gives us the sense of meaning, hope, and dignity that keeps us going, especially when we're facing extreme hardship. Throughout his sentence, there have been very few moments of organizing and rebellion. Most of the years were like a morass, with nearly all the other prisoners either focused on the self-help (or more accurately, *self-blame*) programs the state offers, or the constant whirlpool of petty crime and gang politics that directs violence against other prisoners rather than against the system and the guards. Together, "self-help" and collective self-harm make prisons self-governing, and those in charge make it hell for those who actually want to change things.

Nonetheless, repression is not final. Those in power have been trying to stamp out our resistance for hundreds of years, and we're still here, learning how to resist them and overcome them. We can survive repression and keep going, but it involves adapting to changes. Sometimes, because it can be uncomfortable to confront our weaknesses, we fail to ask the right questions, or we fall into dynamics of avoidance (what Daniel Kahn calls an "internal emigration"). Other times, a wave of repression can be so vicious, we have to surrender the territory we've fought for, leave our home, lose our roots.

It is in these moments—if we fail to bend with the force of repression, or if it temporarily breaks us—that the State can step in for a strategic reset. A reset is like a rupture in the continuity of our struggles, a barrier that prevents the next generation from learning from all the experiences that preceded them. After a reset, the State and its allies can completely alter the conversation, so that everyone who is talking about a social problem is actually perpetuating it, despite their best intentions.

Within these engineered-from-above conversations, people don't ask, *what is the most effective way to abolish the police?* They ask, *what reform will make the police behave?* They don't ask, *what forms of social organization allow us to live in a healthy relationship with our ecology?* They ask, *what politician do we have to vote for, what product do we have to buy, what kind of economic growth is the best, to save the environment?*

White-supremacist, NGO-dominated, middle-class environmentalism grew and thrived in the '70s and '80s, in the years immediately after violent waves of repression against Indigenous, anticapitalist, anticolonial movements. Organizations and individuals who turned their backs on those earlier movements were incorporated into government, academia, and NGOs, often with a fat paycheck, and they helped to falsify the history of what people were struggling for, what they accomplished, and what they learned.

Likewise, throughout the '00s and the '10s, movements that were simultaneously anticolonial, anticapitalist, and ecological were growing across the world. Indigenous struggles in so-called "First World" countries gained a force and visibility they had not had in a long time, particularly at Standing Rock, Black Mesa, Unist'ot'en, and Sápmi.[21] In North America, Indigenous struggles were targeted with extreme repression that, in many cases, put them on the defensive or exacerbated

---

21   The first two places are occupied by the US, the third by Canada, and the fourth, the homeland of the Sámi people (Sápmi is the Sámi people's own name for their traditional territory), is occupied by Norway, Sweden, Finland, and Russia.

internal differences. Meanwhile, in Europe, anticapitalist movements were facing an inflection point. In 2005, 2006, 2008, 2011, 2012, 2014, 2018, and 2019, major European cities like Paris, Athens, Barcelona, London, Madrid, and dozens more were rocked by huge revolts. Many cities experienced rebellions multiple times over these years, and in many cases police were utterly defeated as people temporarily took control of their cities.

However, these revolts and insurrections did not automatically turn into revolutions (we seem to have forgotten that, throughout history, they never have). People faced exhaustion. They also faced an extremely difficult choice about what next steps to take, and most people took the easiest option: avoiding that choice. Movements stalled, shrank, and withered.

And it was in that moment that reformist, colonial, naïve, compartmentalized environmentalism started making a huge comeback in North America and Europe. The prime example of this new, self-defeating direction is Extinction Rebellion (aka XR), which was founded largely by academics and professional activists in the UK at the end of 2018. Just one year later, mainstream media like CNN, owned and funded by many of the major companies responsible for climate change, would be publishing celebratory articles about XR, praising their supposed successes and branding them "the world's fastest growing climate movement."[22]

Heather Luna, a Colombian-USer who spent 17 years in the UK and now lives in Colombia, is an anti-oppression, antiracist facilitator/educator who also supports people harmed by

---

22 Eliza Mackintosh, "A psychedelic journey, a radical strategy and perfect timing," *CNN*, December 25, 2019: www.cnn.com/2019/12/25/uk/extinction-rebellion-gail-bradbrook-gbr-intl/index.html (accessed March 24, 2024).

white, middle-class environmental struggles. As she describes it, the appearance of XR was not a positive development:

Back in 2019, XR would say they were listening to the criticism and issues raised by refugees, immigrants, disabled people, and folks from the working class. But the listening never led to the proposed decolonial approach. They were ego-driven on spreading the brand around the world rather than encouraging local groups to do what made sense to the local culture of struggle and resistance. They drew upon Gandhi and the Civil Rights Movement without an understanding of context, and while ignoring current struggles that demonstrate the "communing" approach.

Anna, the researcher and movement participant who shared about the effects and methods of police repression earlier in this chapter, also pushes back on the mainstream characterization of the climate movement:

I think this loss of collective memory is important to understand the current wave of climate organizing, and the groups that emerged—XR, Just Stop Oil, Insulate Britain ... There's this idea that the last few years has seen the "emergence" of an environmental direct action movement in the UK.

Firstly, this completely invisibilizes the long and rich history of direct action in the UK, of successful organizing. Think of the successful organizing against road building, through forest occupations, tree sits, direct action, physical resistance, community building, and sabotage, especially in the '90s. Seventy-five percent of the government's massive roads expansion projects were never built because of people mobilizing against new projects wherever they were proposed. Hundreds of new roads were cancelled.

Or the fight against GMOs, which were halted (though what victory is ever final?) because people went out during the night or during the day, digging up fields, occupying Monsanto offices, taking diverse forms of direct action against GMO companies ... These were not single-issue campaigns the way they are today, they built movements, social relations, community. This rich history, the lessons learnt, and the political analyses have often been sidelined / ignored, despite attempts from people to have dialogue and conversation.

Secondly, in my eyes, there is a misunderstanding of direct action. What these new movements practice is civil disobedience, appealing to the state to take climate breakdown seriously, or to stop doing things it's doing (like granting new oil and gas licenses).

And within direct action, we see a focus on spectacle, on building an "activist culture, not a culture of resistance," as a friend once called it. And a focus on "arrestability," which becomes almost a yardstick in many circles, according to which your activist credentials are measured, your activist "worth." Of course, this excludes so many people and ends up making this a very white, middle-class movement, approachable to liberals, academics, etc. And it facilitates repression and surveillance.

Thirdly, in my eyes, there is a deep underlying misunderstanding of how the state and its institutions—like the courts—actually work. Ironically, these movements are quite good at showing that as much as we might struggle inside these institutions (like in court cases), they are not sites for positive social change. Yet, that seems to be driving a lot of activism—convincing juries, judges, state institutions whose job it is to protect the status quo. And that comes at a high cost, with people jailed, policed, broken. Imagine if all that energy was channeled into radical, not reformist movements or organizing, anonymous direct action ... movements that challenge state power and capitalism.

The focus on spectacular "activism," the emphasis on intentionally getting arrested and making our arguments in court, the nonviolence, all the self-policing in these new movements: all of this makes repression easier. We're seeing referrals of organisers under PREVENT, the anti-radicalisation programme, we're seeing divide-and-conquer techniques, criminalisation, incarceration ...

And we're seeing new generations of activists burnt out and in jail, and as you say, inventing things from scratch, being unaware of our histories, lessons learnt, strategies developed. Many are scared into action, by catastrophic messaging focused on carbon emissions and apocalypse narratives. I don't think this type of messaging is very helpful sometimes; it's not empowering and it lacks political analysis. The absolute blindness to colonialism is just the most obvious example, and the carbon reductionism leads to a disregard for carbon colonialism, for ecologies and ecosystems that might be destroyed under the name of mitigation.

The Road

The highway bridge that Charles described occupying in an anti-police protest in Chapter 1 was built on top of what had been an important Black community. Much of the neighborhood was destroyed in the construction.

Ominously, the interstate highway system in the US, or motorways in the UK, are the importation of a Nazi contribution to the field of national engineering: the *Autobahn*.[23] We can use the theoretical framework of *social war* to understand how the highway system was a technological advancement organized strategically by the State to simultaneously achieve multiple, mutually reinforcing objectives, like speeding up military mobilizations both to quell internal rebellions, or to carry out surprise, rapid invasions of neighboring countries. The highway system increases a central government's power to intervene as the architect of society in other ways as well: by generating economic growth to provide fuel to the whole social machine, and by further alienating a population in a way that makes them easier to govern. Highways and their associated car culture are in fact an integral part of the major forms of capital accumulation and social alienation that sky-rocketed in the twentieth century.

On a highway, you can have a crowd of people who are all completely alone, *incommunicado*. This is, of course, one of the most important cultural phenomena of the last fifty years: the traffic jam, thousands of people, side by side, *with the same interests*, in the same situation, yet anti-solidaristic, entirely

---

23   In another example of how there is frequently continuity and similarity between democratic and fascist states, the idea original-ly stems from the Weimar Republic, but few construction projects got the support they needed until Hitler was elected: after that, the *Autobahn* system took off. And they were modeled on an earlier am-bitious project of the modern State: the railroads. In *The Solutions Are Already Here*, I look at how the railroads are a useful topic for understanding the concept of social war, as they were strategically designed to simultaneously act as a colonial instrument of genocide against Indigenous peoples in the Great Plains, an ecocidal infra-structure, an important contribution to warfare logistics, an engine of commerce and production, and a delivery mechanism for the rap-id settling of the occupied West Coast.

isolated, unable to communicate, either ignoring one another, or annoyed with everyone. A triumph of capitalism.

Today, highways are what they use to transport the National Guard to crush our rebellions when we take over a city. Sometimes, we take over highways and blockade them, since they are the lifeblood of a deadly economy. But, by design, they are difficult terrain to defend, and many of us have been hurt on highways, when the police throw us off overpasses, when cop cars or angry drivers run us over.

Memory does not just live in our brains. In fact, our minds are much larger than our brains: our memory and thinking processes also live in our friendships, families, and intimate partnerships, and they live in our surroundings. People with healthy relationships show improved recall in studies when they are asked to remember information collectively rather than individually. Being able to order our own living space also helps us to think and remember clearly, especially if our living space is allowed to extend beyond a house or apartment and into the surrounding neighborhood. If we're forced to move every few years as the prices go up, if the buildings, gardens, and forests we grew up around are demolished or built over, this is also an erasure of memory.

When governments have the power to decide what neighborhoods should be demolished or defunded; when governments decide which neighborhoods can be turned into engines of profit by declaring they have "cultural value," when they decide which buildings and parks, forests, or rivers should be designated protected monuments, and what artifacts of history to put in a museum, they control our historical memory as surely as when they design the school curriculum. Even worse, through these mechanisms of dispossession and alienation, they destroy collective memory—the ability to narrate, embody, and pass on our own memories—leaving us without the roots or relationships necessary to understand our place in the world.

Construction mega-projects uproot us from an intimate territory, destroy that territory, and give the State a blank slate, an opportunity to design what can be referred to broadly as *a prison architecture*. If the State and the wealthy, who have a vested interest in ruling us and exploiting us, have the opportunity to design the spaces we carry out our lives in, they will design spaces that make us easier to control, easier to surveil, and fully dependent on them for our survival.

Construction mega-projects can take on the forms of major highway construction, the demolition and reconstruction of entire neighborhoods with the justification of "urban renewal," giant hydroelectric dams funded by the IMF to promote "economic development" in the "developing world," and now a huge wave of "green energy" projects that destroy immense swathes of territory, making investors a great deal of money without actually slowing the increase of greenhouse gas emissions.

It is no coincidence that these mega-projects, which bring together the combined force of states and international investors, frequently target lower-class and racialized neighborhoods that were the sites of historical resistance, or that are the homes of communities that still enjoy some degree of autonomy from State and Capital.

Major hydroelectric dams built in the second half of the twentieth century flooded the homelands of millions of traditionally stateless people, from Central America to Iraq to India and China. In the United States, interstate highway construction subsidized by the federal government systematically targeted and destroyed Black neighborhoods. Just as the Supreme Court struck down legal segregation—a major victory for the movement against racism—the federal government was preparing "Housing and Urban Development" grants to intentionally demolish Black neighborhoods and create made-to-police housing projects. Cynically, they did this in the name of fighting poverty and discrimination, another hand-out to the movements that thought a white-su-premacist, capitalist system could be reformed.

In Harrisonburg, the town in Virginia where I lived for the first six years of my adult life, a HUD grant funded the demolition of the Black and Jewish neighborhood, which had been right next to downtown. Just over ten years after the Holocaust, the Jewish cemetery was forcibly relocated "up the hill," and Black neighbors were put into the projects, housing blocs that were easy to surveil, removed from any cultural center or comfortable gathering place, and devoid of any neighborhood-owned businesses. All the Black businesses were destroyed, and the *only* business in the original neighborhood that was rebuilt and continues to exist to this day (or at least, it was still there the last time I visited), just so happened to be the *only* white business, the ice cream parlor.

Almost no one who lives in Harrisonburg today knows this history, invisible yet just beneath their feet. And I only learned about it when a friend and I interviewed a local Black elder to talk about the history of racism and Black resistance in the town for our anarchist radio show.

Rarely do people manage to stop these projects, but when we do, the significance of our victories is lost if we cannot remember them from one decade to the next.

In the 1960s, planners in the UK proposed a series of ring roads around London that would have demolished a large part of Brixton, which since the '40s and '50s was a largely Afro-Caribbean neighborhood and already a hot spot for anti-police and antiracist rebellions. All the demolitions required by the ring-road construction would have displaced 100,000 households, while stealing the sense of neighborhood from many more, with the loss of parks, shops, and gathering places, and the imposition of towering, noisy, poisonous highways.

In 1970, "Homes before Roads" formed to stop the project. This was a flash point in the growth of movements opposing a destructive wave of road construction. As we heard in the interview with Anna above, 75 percent of new road projects were cancelled, and hundreds of these roads and highways were never built. Brixton, for one, was largely saved.

Also as we heard, the spread of environmentalist NGOs and mass organizations like Extinction Rebellion is directly predicated on forgetting these struggles. No one would act the fool, flying to big official conferences or making a bunch of political theater for shameless politicians and ruthless financial institutions, if they remembered those institutions were rooted in slavery and if they accepted what our relationship with them has always been. More so if they remembered that we have won meaningful victories in the past, and it was not with exclusively nonviolent, media-driven tactics in single-issue campaigns.

In fact, one of the strengths of the anti-roads movement was how it was a movement of intersections. Many of its origin points were antiracist and working class. These were not large landlords trying to protect the value of their holdings; they were people fighting for their homes, their neighborhoods, and in rural areas, their access to the commons. They gained a great deal of strength from antiracist movements that stood up against other manifestations of white supremacy, from police killings to extreme forms of labor exploitation and deportations targeting racialized people. And antiracism in the UK, in turn, had learned and grown from the anticolonial struggles in India, Africa, and the Caribbean in the preceding decades.

Many rural people who participated in the anti-roads movement drew inspiration from the quiet, centuries-long war of resistance to protect the commons from enclosure. Highways showed up as just the latest form of enclosure, a more catastrophic version of an aristocrat throwing up a fence to try to appropriate a meadow, marsh, or forest. And because the struggle against enclosure had long used techniques of sabotage and of clandestinity, or at least discretion, the anti-roads movement inherited that tactical knowledge when they went after construction sites and machinery.

There were also movements of cultural and spiritual rebellion against the entire society of domination, like the travelers who revived a tradition of unpermitted free festivals at Stonehenge every summer solstice. In 1985, at the Battle of the Beanfield, hundreds of police attacked, injuring and arresting everyone they could, to crush the attempt to create new ways of living.

Another manifestation of this resistance erupted with Reclaim the Streets, which began in London around 1995 and subsequently spread to other cities and countries. Reclaim the Streets is a very joyous, festive, and illegal blending of desires, needs, and tactics. It exists on a spectrum of roving dance party, unpermitted protest with food, music, and kids' activities, illegal rave, and riot with a sound system. People come to Reclaim the Streets out of a desire to transform the urban space they live in, oppose car culture, reassert the commons, attack gentrification, and enjoy a free, non-commercialized culture. It is a lively example of intersectional struggle deploying diverse tactics, an anticolonial and lower-class take on environmentalism, and joyful resistance.

Stop me if you've heard this one before: Reclaim the Streets was not a new phenomenon, but a seemingly spontaneous eruption that drew on the methods of earlier generations, like the Stop the City protest carnivals of 1983 and 1984 that blockaded the City, London's financial district, as a way of targeting war profiteering and the military industrial complex. This earlier wave of protest, in its own time, had grown from a mixing of the persistent anti-nuclear movement and the growing anarcho-punk and squatting movements. Though Stop the City brought together a wide range of struggles, from anti-militarism and anti-apartheid to feminism and animal liberation, it constrained its effectiveness through an adherence to performance-based nonviolence, and stagnated in siloed, subcultural scenes rather than breaking through to a more expansive intersectionality.

The Fork

Indigenous liberation movements bring something incomparable to the table because they, better than anyone, can tell the origin story of the institutions of power that currently rule the world. They fight for recognition of the history of conquest, and make it undeniable that conquest is the basis for ownership of the land and for the power of the institutions that govern us. And though every Indigenous society is unique, together they carry the collective memory of entirely other ways to live and to relate, the knowledge that capitalism, the State, and patriarchy are not necessary.

People who no longer remember who they were before colonialism, whether these are people trapped in whiteness or another national identity that has been statist, colonial, and deterritorialized for as long as anyone can remember, can contribute to anticolonial struggles by changing the course of their own history and developing an ecocentric social relation that places solidarity above loyalty to any state or any colonizing culture.

Around the world, Indigenous communities are on the frontline against both fossil fuel extraction and green energy mega-projects, like cobalt mining in Central Africa and massive wind farms in Oaxaca. Their resistance questions who has access to the land, how they got that access, and what the results are of their treatment of the land. Both their history and current forms of organization prove that it is capitalism that actually needs fuel and electricity on such a massive scale.

In North America, the Wet'suwet'en, Lakota, Ojibwe, Diné, and other peoples, together with their allies, have been fighting to block a wide range of construction projects that would destroy and desecrate their lands. At Standing Rock, an eleven-month-long encampment from April 2016 to February 2017, together with prayer ceremonies, marches, protests, blockades, popular education, and sabotage, stopped the Dakota Access pipeline.[24] In the months and years immediately following, numerous pipeline and mining projects around the continent have been scrapped after early signs of resistance, because investors have come to understand how difficult anticolonial movements can make it for them to complete their projects, even with the backing of the government, police, and militaries.

None of these movements have been simple experiences, though.

Klee Benally, the Diné writer, musician, and anarchist, describes the resistance at Standing Rock which drew "hundreds of Indigenous nations with thousands of water

---

24 When Trump came into office a few weeks later, the federal government pushed it through again, and it is likely that the Obama administration knew that would be the case, but were trying to score political points by temporarily halting construction, symbolically placing guilt for the project on Republicans.

protectors and land defenders who came willing to risk their lives to protect the Lakota sacred site from oil pipeline dese-cration."There was a great deal of internal conflict, though, as various NGOs and Indigenous politicians "parachuted in" or "embedded themselves in the camps and structured the politi-cal campaigns in alignment with their pre-existing strategies." The official "Tribal Council, nonprofits, and some elders, established themselves as colonial proxies, or 'movement police,' aiding the cops by working against actions employed by our people. They removed barricades, doused fires, and physically blocked acts of resistance on the frontlines":[25]

> On any night around one fire you'd have White Mountain Ndee' singing and dancing with Havusupai relatives and Hopi sharing pikki bread, and around another fire you'd have conspiratorial young forces planning their next daring action, at another you'd have would-be white saviors imposing themselves [...] The social power was undeniable, everyone could feel it suspended in the tense air.[26]

While their "colonial proxies" inside the movement tried to pacify or blame more radical sectors, the government capi-talized on the growing tensions to enact vicious repression, mobilizing local police, federal agents, and also private merce-naries employing counterterrorism measures they had learned in the US neocolonial wars in Iraq and Afghanistan. They used military hardware, paid informants, and also the weather, spraying resisters with water in the sub-zero temperatures of

---

25 Klee Benally, *No Spiritual Surrender: Indigenous Anarchy in Defense of the Sacred*, Detritus Books, 2023, pp.95, 96–97, and 100.
26 Benally, *No Spiritual Surrender*, p.97.

winter on the Great Plains. Hundreds of people were injured, many of them permanently.

Despite such intense repression, the resistance has continued, teaching us another important lesson: it is important not to make our enemies seem stronger than they actually are. As one Lakota friend told me, colonialism "hasn't succeeded, because I'm still here."

The persistence she is hinting at is vital. Not far from Standing Rock, the Lakota tried to win back their freedom in several battles in the early '70s. In 1973, Oglala Lakota and the American Indian Movement (AIM) reclaimed Wounded Knee on the Pine Ridge Lakota reservation. They held their own against police and paramilitaries, though three resisters were killed. Later, in 1975, they killed two FBI agents who were invading Lakota lands to orchestrate paramilitary violence. Most police and paramilitaries, however, faced no consequences. The repression was stifling, with 64 unsolved deaths in and around the reservation, and many AIM members and sympathizers imprisoned, including Leonard Peltier, who is still behind bars.

The movement pivoted and shifted focus, but it is still here. The emphasis on survival and memory contributes to effective adaptation in times of intense repression: when the war gets too hot, find a path of less resistance, gain strength, learn lessons, and then find another moment to go on the offensive again.

The resistance at Pine Ridge, and AIM itself, came after decades of organizing for survival, defeating the attempts of the US and Canadian governments to assimilate Indigenous peoples by destroying their languages, spirituality, and historical memory. One of the first offensives of that generation came with the 1969 reclamation of Alcatraz Island by the group, Indians of All Nations. Their action, which led to a

19-month inhabitation of the island, pointed to the possibilities of self-organization and transformation, as an infamous abandoned prison was turned into a living community, with a clinic, kitchen, school, and radio. The movement also centered the historical memory of colonization by creating a visible reminder that the continent was taken by force. Throughout their action, Indians of All Nations referred back to their history, with sarcastic claims that Alcatraz belonged to them by right of discovery, or offers to buy the island back from the government with a few dollars worth of glass beads.

The subversive transformation of Alcatraz can provide a critical comparison when we examine the transformation at another place of suffering. Angola prison, in Louisiana, is infamous for its racism and brutality. Through the end of the Civil War, it was a plantation where wealthy whites and their middle managers and overseers enslaved, tortured, and exploited kidnapped Africans and their descendants.

Its transition from plantation to prison was rather simple. When slavery was abolished, the government used methods like prison to force Black people to work.

The celebration of Juneteenth—the abolition of slavery in the United States—stems from the June 19, 1865 proclamation in Galveston, Texas, which was the last holdout amongst the slave states. Significantly, Juneteenth does not center Black people who fought against slavery, like those who set up communes of fugitives and guerrilla fighters in the Carolina lowlands.

On the contrary, the holiday centers a white authority figure, on a stage, addressing a passive audience. This is what Major General Gordon Granger said that day in Galveston:

The people of Texas are informed that, in accordance with a proclamation from the Executive of the United

States, all slaves are free. This involves an absolute equality of personal rights and rights of property between former masters and slaves, and the connection heretofore existing between them becomes that between employer and hired labor. The freedmen are advised to remain *quietly* at their present homes and work for wages. They are informed that they will not be allowed to collect at military posts and that they will not be supported in idleness either there or elsewhere.[27]

Simultaneous to the abolition of slavery, forced labor was legalized against people convicted of a crime. And as Granger indicated, "idleness" (not working for their former masters) could itself be considered a crime. We should also remember that "equal rights" under the democratic system means that rich people and poor people have the same right to invest their money, to collect interest on loans, to work for wages, to own land, to sell and buy and rent things. We also see an immediate signal of the unequal application of this meaningless form of equality: the reference to military posts meant that freed Blacks could not appeal for government aid.

In this light, abolition was primarily a change in accounting practices: under democracy and capitalism, Black people were given nothing to make up for the past. They were given their freedom along with absolute poverty, so they had to work for their former masters in exchange for money to pay for low-quality food and housing, rather than working and directly being provided with low-quality food and housing.

Additionally, Black people were prohibited from gathering in groups. Similar prohibitions remained in force for the next

27 Quoted from Clint Smith, *How the Word Is Passed*, New York: Back Bay Books, 2021, pp.173–174; emphasis mine.

several years across the South, a crucial time for the State to transform one white supremacist regime into another.

Poor whites were also forced to work in this new prison regime, unlike their wealthy counterparts. Black people were imprisoned, and still are imprisoned, at hugely disproportionate rates; nonetheless, imprisonment could have been a cause for more solidarity against racial capitalism. However, many progressive, Christian whites had long seen some form of prison as an acceptable method for reformation, far superior to corporal and capital punishment. Prison was designed, at least putatively, to teach the disorderly lower classes proper habits of work and discipline. And other whites were distracted by patriotic, religious, and nationalist allegiances based on false histories: they had been tricked into thinking the ruling class was on their side because they had the same skin color and practiced the same religion.

Nonetheless, abolition was also a huge achievement. In the following decades, Black people fought to turn Juneteenth into a celebration of their freedom, though a Black newspaper in Houston wrote in 1941, "Negroes are not sure whether to be gay on 'Juneteenth' or to observe the day with sadness. They do not know whether they are actually free here."

White supremacy adapted and thrived, but this only makes the struggle for memory all the more vital. Clint Smith, whose research I am drawing on in these paragraphs, describes "a paralysis that had arisen from never knowing enough of my own history to effectively identify the lies I was being told." He goes on to express the importance of "[u]nderstanding that all this was done not by accident but by design. That did not strip me of agency, it gave agency back to me."[28]

---

28 The three quotes from this and the preceding paragraph are from Clint Smith, *How the Word Is Passed*, pp.188, 178, and 179.

If more people remembered this history—that abolition was already achieved once, but in a way perfectly compatible with white supremacy—what changes would they make as they fight for abolition a second time?

William C. Anderson and Joy James are two of many voices that bring a sharp analysis to this debate:

> Not everyone who says they're an abolitionist even knows what the term means. Its increasing popularity risks stripping it of all meaning. If we allow it to become co-opted, it could easily become a reinvented version of reformism. According to Joy James, this narrowing of the meaning of abolition is "the logical conclusion of deradicalizing the prison struggle by severing it from a grassroots, working-class, Black base or people of color base that sought autonomy from the state."[29]

Instead of promoting some new reform, Anderson argues that abolition needs to take aim at the roots of oppression:

> The lie that we live in a great, equitable democracy damages countless people who are forced to carry the weight of this myth. Believing that this is the best version of a society, as it claims to be, transforms our hardships, our poverty, and unhappiness into something that's our own fault. This is a deadly lie. How this country was created and how it continues to function will destroy us

---

For the first quote, Smith cites Elizabeth H. Turner, "Juneteenth: Emancipation and Memory," in *Lone Star Pasts: Memory and History in Texas*, eds. Gregg Cantrell and Elizabeth H. Turner, College Station: Texas A&M University Press, 2007, p.162.

29 Anderson, *The Nation on No Map; Black Anarchism and Abolition*, pp.36–37, also quoting Joy James' May 6, 2019 talk at Brown University, "The Architects of Abolitionism."

all if we don't expand the work to abolish it as soon as possible. It's not just the police, the Supreme Court, the Senate, or the military: the entirety of this fatal project must be brought to an end.[30]

While conducting research for my previous book, I came across the infuriating but unsurprising fact that the NGOs making big salaries talking about human rights and the environment don't count the deaths of land defenders who fight back. Every year, lists are compiled of all the environmentalists and land defenders around the world who are murdered by police or paramilitaries when they go up against multinational companies like the Dole Food Company, ExxonMobil, or mining companies supplying for Tesla and Apple. But if they fight the police, carry out sabotage, or pick up arms, their deaths literally are not counted.

No one can deny that poor, rural, and Indigenous communities around the world are facing extermination. And yet, seemingly respectable humanitarians deny them a right to survival and self-defense.

Also during my research, I came across some developments in the struggle against the oil industry in Nigeria. I had been impacted by the story of this resistance when I was 13 and I found out, in real time, about the execution of Ken Saro-Wiwa and other Ogoni activists resisting Shell Oil. A decade later, the Movement for the Emancipation of the Niger Delta (MEND) appeared, a primarily Ijaw group that had declared war on the oil industry, demanding the dismantling of drilling sites and pipelines so that Ijaw communities could feed themselves through traditional agricultural practices.

---

30   Anderson, *The Nation on No Map*, p.4.

I found this struggle inspiring. Impoverished peoples have every right to demand control of the profits made from resources extracted from their lands, and the likes of Shell and Chevron have enriched themselves, while keeping Nigeria polluted and in poverty. Nonetheless, such an approach creates a divergence between people's short-term and long-term possibilities for survival. Industries like petroleum eventually become everyone's problem, so movements that seek to abolish such industries, fighting instead for food security through autonomy and the healing of the land, are choosing a more farsighted path.

When I looked them up later, though, I saw that MEND had taken a turn towards Christian nationalism after serious conflicts in Nigeria involving Boko Haram.[31] In 2013, they threatened to bomb mosques and assassinate Muslim clerics. Though they shifted course after receiving criticism, and I have little idea how the movement has evolved since then, the turn towards nationalism and authoritarian methods certainly resembles a common pattern.

Within this society, resistance inevitably leads us to a fork in the road, a bifurcation in our choices.

---

31 Boko Haram is a Sunni jihadist organization based in northern Nigeria and also active in neighboring countries. Their official name denotes an adherence to the concepts of *dawah* and *jihad*, which in their case can be translated as "proselytism and holy war," though these words can take on very different meanings for most other Muslims. The latter word, for example, can be understood as "struggle or self-sacrifice for a worthy cause." Boko Haram seeks the overthrow of the Nigerian government, and the eradication of Shia Muslims as well as non-Muslims, like the many Christians and animists who also live in Nigeria and neighboring countries. They have carried out numerous massacres and mass kidnappings, particularly against schoolchildren.

When we give up on mere protest, we will encounter one or another preconceived model for change, ready and waiting for us, offering us resources to make a difference.

The model we encounter may be the NGOs. They'll tell us: *go to college, dress nicely, learn how to speak like a professional, repeat these talking points, organize these unpaid volunteers to get signatures and donations, go to this conference, put together this PowerPoint, lobby these politicians* ... You might only end up weakening and betraying real social movements, but if you play your cards right, you'll make a much higher salary than you would waiting tables, driving a cab, teaching, translating, cleaning, writing ...

Or, if we live in another part of the world, maybe we'll encounter a political party with an armed wing, ready to recruit us. The issues they are raising might be valid, but the stronger they get, the more they take advantage of the resources offered to them by neighboring states, by international agencies, by global media. Those resources come with strings, and there are serious expectations around what they can achieve, how they should act. With enough good fortune, good strategy, good allies, and bloodshed, they may overthrow the current government and take charge (either in a coup or by pressuring for elections they can win). They may even win recognition as a new state. Coincidentally, though, it won't be very different from the old state ...

This is how the capitalist world system works. If you are a nation-state, you are allowed to use force, and if you want to be taken seriously as a new ruling class or a new nation-state, you need a capable military, good negotiators, and you have to play by the rules. If you are not a government or proto-government, you are a civilian, and there are other rules to play by: elections, advertising, messaging, education.

A huge part of the global economy goes into conditioning people that this is how change works. If people are not forced down a single path, but instead are offered a constrained choice and promised resources if they accept any of the options laid out before them, then few people will refuse to follow the roads already constructed by the system.

Movements that seek change outside of this system will be treated like criminals and terrorists, and that actually holds true regardless of whether they are a dozen friends fighting to save their urban garden, or to stop the clearcutting of a nearby forest, or if they are ten thousand people fighting for the cultural, linguistic, and ecological survival of their society.

The State will try to eradicate people who refuse either established path when they come to this fork in the road. The goal is to erase them, to make sure they are never remembered. Meanwhile, those who embrace one of the paths of (least) resistance offered to them can do so sincerely, because they are unaware of their own history. This is systematic: in order to be successful, NGO directors pulling in six- and seven-figure salaries, and party leaders making decisions for entire liberation movements have to be able to effectively suppress or distort the memory of how they betrayed the cause, favoring their own self-interests, choosing the pragmatic calculations of power politics, allowing themselves to be bribed and bought off by the dominant system.

CHAPTER 3

But We Are Here, Surviving, Remembering, Passing On The Torch

From a young age I was close to the social movements because my mother and my father took part in struggles, in their own time and in their own ways. When I started studying at the university (which I later gave up), my compas *and I created a student assembly in which we began discussing different struggles, local problems, and more global problems. We got to know other groups of different political tendencies who were active in our city, but little by little we were tending towards anarchism as a guide for our ethics and our praxis.*

As the months went by, we got wrapped up in a diversity of struggles against the price hike in public transportation, demands for justice for the massacres committed by the Mexican State in previous years, also a student strike in the universities. The State responded to all of this with extremely violent repression, which pushed us to organize ourselves for street fighting. We organized so that we could fight in Black Blocs. In the beginning, these were purely defensive, enabling us to contain the police who were beating us.

Around this time, there was a change in the government due to an electoral fraud that brought lots of people to the capital to try to stop the new president from taking power, and although we do not and we will not ever participate in the dynamics of governmental power, we saw it as an opportunity to meet other groups from around the country who like ourselves were fighting in the streets, and not just in legal ways like well behaved citizens. This was how we met other anarchist groups with whom we started forming links, with their frictions and conflicts, but also growing and discussing a great deal.

Later on, in our own area, a mining company tried to set up near a major energy plant. We participated in the resistance, which was the first time we came into direct confrontation with paramilitaries, drug traffickers, and the irregular forces of the State. The repression kept growing, so we also escalated our tactics. Now we weren't only painting graffiti on the walls in the hours before dawn, but also starting to set fire to police cars and carry out acts of sabotage against the mining company that had its headquarters in the capital of our local state.

This brought us closer to the struggles of the First Nations and also the environmental struggle (always the anticapitalist tendency thereof).

We fought against the construction of a major dam that a foreign company—a big Brazilian conglomerate—tried to install on a river close to our city. The dam would have caused the destruction of several villages and it would have permanently altered the landscape, as well as being for the sole benefit of the businesses and the wealthy, displacing people and degrading the land. This struggle was carried out behind barricades that were constantly attacked by the Mexican Army.

One year later, there was a massacre in which 43 students were killed, which led to many of us in the street organizing ourselves in a way that was now less defensive and more offensive. The struggle began to take a less public and more clandestine character, so we could protect our identities and stay safe. With the escalation of the conflict, several of us had to flee and live underground for several years. In my case, I went to live in a village where they were fighting against the wind energy companies that were taking over their lands. Our mutual friend had to flee the country because of death threats, but I stayed.

In this village, there were intense battles, one where eleven of us were injured by live ammunition. After a time, I moved to the federal capital, México City, where I worked with a publishing group. With several other compas, *we prepared a series of actions against the banks, companies, and armed forces of the State.*

Later, I went back to the town, which was calmer now, since the companies had given up their development project in that particular area. But then a health problem almost killed me off and I had to go back to my hometown where I had the networks of support I needed to recover.

It took me almost a year to recover my health. When the pandemic arrived, because of a lack of resources for all our projects, I migrated to work in the north of the country, but it almost destroyed me emotionally.

In our reflections (very similar to your own), the counterinsurgency opens up gaps between the generations, so the State can win the race for people's hearts and minds. We found that for this to work, peace is built out of a great many mental chains. "Our chains are in our minds," we concluded one day, and we began to prepare our struggle to go more and more on the offensive, on the offensive against forgetting, the forgetting of other struggles and other forms of existence. We saw that they weren't only trying to eliminate the pueblos[32] *and the dissident movements, but also*

---

32   In Spanish, "*pueblos*" refers simultaneously to "peoples" and in this context, Indigenous peoples, and also to villages. Many Indigenous cultures have a strong identification with rurality, with a mode of living based around a reciprocal relationship with the land, such that those who move away from the *pueblos* might identify as Indigenous but "from the city."

to eliminate anything they can't control. That's why I'm telling you all this. To remember that the knowledge that we can fight is something that should be spread, universalized.

The counterinsurgency in my city became a part of the landscape: demolishing the oldest squatted social center to build a parking lot. Redesigning the communal dining hall we set up in the university and that was open to everyone, to turn it into a cafeteria that was exclusive to students. And our own dead were claimed by the institutions and rewritten as activists and good citizens.

As people of the city we don't have memory of our roots, and in the villages, the social war motivates people to move to the city to live a modern urban, Western life. The State commemorates the struggles it can assimilate, take advantage of, or use to its favor, while the scars and cracks we are able to inflict on it, the State passes off as anomalies and covers up with cosmetics.

This interview was with an anarchist "born in the territory dominated by the Mexican state." For his own safety, he asked to do the interview anonymously.

The theme of continuity arises again and again in this *compa*'s experience. Its manifestations might appear familiar or alien to us: growing up with parents who participated in earlier struggles and still talked about them; going on the offensive after confronting and surviving repression; learning a new relationship to history after struggling alongside Indigenous movements with an anticolonial perspective; going on the run to avoid police; changing the intensity of one's involvement because of economic need and health problems, but then being able to come back to the struggle.

Many of us have come to expect that each new generation will grow up unaware of the struggles that preceded them, having to make all the same mistakes and to learn similar versions of the same lessons. But what if it doesn't have to be that way?

Accompaniment or Loss

There is a widespread feeling in nearly all the movements I have participated in. I'm not sure there's a word for it. We can call it "avoidant loss": the commonplace acceptance that we will lose people in the course of our resistance, that we have already lost many people, but that it's best not to talk about it.

This loss is often considered final, as though certain friends and comrades no longer exist. They have been *disappeared*. Sometimes, this disappearance is the result of something called "burnout": at a certain point: people just get tired and leave. Actually, the people who supposedly leave or disappear are responding directly to ableism or patriarchy or other harmful behaviors they experience at the hands of comrades, because of unhealthy practices around conflict and emotions, or even because they've shifted to other types of activity and other focuses of liberation and transformation. Who the hell decided that certain actions are not a part of the movement, not a form of struggle? More importantly, why do many of us continue to reinforce this separation?

The term itself should have clued us in. Living beings do not *burn out*. Fuses in a machine burn out. And we are not machines. Capitalism wants to treat us like machines. We should not reproduce its logic.

For the most part, though, we use the term without looking at it, and so those who *burn out*—defective fuses—are thrown into the same box where we discard those who have gone to prison, those who have died, those who have gotten old. They are gone. Lost. Beyond the pale. And as we lose them, we lose their memory, their experiences, their skills, their failings, their stories, their strength, their imperfections, and their warmth.

But what if no one were truly gone? What if the only ones who were lost were those of us who believed we could ever lose a comrade who had dedicated their life, or even a part of their life, to our collective liberation? What if *we* are the ones having trouble finding our way back to the struggle?

"No one dies but those who are forgotten."

I came across this assertion in a video a friend from the Chilean state sent me, while I was in the midst of writing this book. La C— joined the struggle under the dictatorship and stayed in it through the transition to democracy, part of the large current that turned away from the authoritarian Left and towards anarchism. In the video, a small armed group has taken over a street in front of a prison. They hold a banner commemorating a fallen comrade, shoot off fireworks and a gun, and when the video stops recording, presumably, beat a hasty exit.

No one dies but those who are forgotten. Another way to say this might be: *we all exist through our relations.* We never lose our elders, our loved ones, our comrades. But we are losing relationships, connections. With each perceived loss, we need to ask ourselves: what actually destroyed this relationship? What did I do that is allowing memory to die? How can we respond otherwise to the things that destroy us, so that we grow instead of shrinking? How can we keep these relationships and these memories alive, through all the turbulence of repression, of scarcity, and of life itself?

An anticolonial lens forces us to see this loss in its historical context, without absolving us of the responsibility to change how all the old patterns play out this next time.

Prison and the police exist to steal people away from us, which makes repression one of the clearest moments for realizing that we never actually *lose* our comrades unless we fail to keep those relationships alive. And yet, the feminized labor of support falls disproportionately on just a few shoulders, often family members and romantic partners. The unacknowledged burden of being somebody's lifeline makes it harder for support people to participate in other movement activities, or to step back and take care of themselves. They become alienated, forced to live through an entirely different experience of struggle from the people around them.

Especially without strong support that can act as a bridge, it is difficult to find ways to aid the movement when you're in prison or on the run. Even more difficult is getting out, when you don't know how to integrate your experiences from the inside, when people are afraid to talk with you about it, and when the very existence of prison is ignored on the outside. It's even harder because, once you're in, you can't help but see how the outside is just super-minimum security: *As long as there are bars, we are behind them.*

Prison is never just a punishment of individuals convicted of crimes. It is an act of war against all of us and against memory itself. When someone you care about is locked up, a part of you is locked up with them. I spoke with the brother of an anarchist who was imprisoned for years under serious charges as a result of an FBI set-up specifically targeting the movement. He described it this way:

Your loved one is taken, your family is torn apart, everyone taking turns acting out in pain, trying to support each other without knowing how, or becoming distant. Visitation is a place where everyone puts on a front, no one cries in the visitation room. Correspondence is fiery, you

express the love for each other that couldn't be spoken
in person, but after some years your letters are from different worlds, neither of you can relate to each other
anymore. Separation is a slow death. Now you really
know what it means to have an enemy: the people who
keep this prison system running. There are tens of thousands of them with the support of millions more. When
you see their inhumanity, you know it's never wrong to
attack this enemy, but above all it's the idea that must
be killed.

Jenny has been involved in anti-repression/prisoner support
work since 2006 when her partner was federally indicted and
sentenced to almost twenty years in prison. She was a founding
member of the Tilted Scales Collective and has contributed
to several books on repression, prisoner support and legal
defense, including *A Tilted Guide to Being a Defendant and
Representing Radicals: A Guide for Lawyers and Movements*:

The day-to-day reality of loving someone who is in
prison is a grinding reminder of how effective police
repression and prison are at swallowing people up. The
lack of control, the not knowing, the complete inability
to communicate with your loved one about things both
critically important and mind-numbingly mundane—all
of these eat away at you and create a constant state of
anxiety and dread. If your loved one doesn't call when
you expect them to it could mean that the prison is on
lockdown, or that they have been thrown in the SHU
["special housing units" aka solitary confinement], or
that the move got messed up and they weren't able
to make a call, or that they have been assaulted, or
that they've been moved to a different prison entirely
(maybe one where they are unreachable by you). All of

these possibilities feel equally real in those moments—even when your head tells you they are not. And the realization that the prison controls all of this, and there is nothing you or your loved one inside can do about it, can sometimes make your loved one feel impossibly far away.

There were certainly times when it felt like I was incredibly isolated—because of all the stress and responsibilities of support work but also because having a loved one inside can feel like such a singular experience. There are few things one can honestly compare it to, so that sense of "no one understands what I'm going through" can feel very real in the harder moments. There are, of course, people who do understand—people who also have loved ones in prison. Talking to those folks was one of the best ways I found connection and support. Still, it can feel hard to explain to the people at your workplace why you are in tears just because you missed a phone call, or to your friends why you can't go out at a certain time on a certain day because you might miss a phone call, or to your family why suddenly the holidays don't feel so great, or to your boss why you need every other weekend off so you can drive seven hours each way for a visit with your loved one. Loving someone in prison alters so many things about your life—things big and small, things everyone will notice and things you hardly notice yourself (but that are surely eating away at you, all the same).

Sometimes it feels like you live in an alternate reality. This all sounds very dramatic and I don't mean for it to be. It's not as if we cease living or functioning. But it is no exaggeration to say that this impacts every facet of your life. You carry it with you everywhere you go and there is almost never a moment when you are not thinking about it. Because even after the state swallows someone whole ... it can still get worse. They can lose their phone calls or visits, they can get moved (potentially across the country, in the federal system), they could get hurt or sick and be left to the abysmal care of the medical system inside the Bureau of Prisons, which has a notoriously horrifying track record.

Eric had really amazing support, but doing this on the regular was an exhausting task and not one that I or his local support crew could keep doing indefinitely. It can be incredibly hard to maintain that kind of momentum over the course of years or decades. There are so many reasons for that—the world changes and other things start to take priority, people who were around when the arrest happened drift away, new people drift in and know nothing of the story ...

For us the most challenging time was actually after Eric got out of prison. It is so easy for folks to feel celebratory at this time—and there is good reason for that. But it is also such a challenging and tenuous time. People leaving prison need housing and a job. They need money to buy clothes and groceries and household items and maybe even a car. They need systems of support to help them navigate bureaucracies and learn how to use cell phones. Mostly, they need help navigating new social structures and dynamics, which may make different demands on them than they did ten years ago. So many things change so quickly these days. When people are locked up for years, it's almost as if they are on a different planet. They know things are changing in the world outside the walls but they have no way of knowing the textures and contours of those changes. I think so many people who get out want to stay plugged in to their communities—especially people like Eric who felt so incredibly supported by his community while he was inside—but often their communities forget about them. And I think at that point we do start losing some of our history and collective memory.

We need these stories. Because these stories are made of people. People who taught us so much and fought so hard. People who deserve to be remembered and whose stories are suffused with lessons critical to our understanding of where we come from, where we are going, and how we might get there.

Prison is just one structure that is designed to isolate us by strangling the relationships between us. This follows a larger pattern of how oppressive systems push those trapped within them to reproduce the logic of oppression. Even movements truly based on a belief in liberation can absorb oppressive logics and become a hostile place. This frequently impacts sexual and gender rebels who make up a vital part of the struggle for liberation across the world.

Piro Subrat is a historian specializing in the intersection between the Left and sexual dissidence in the Spanish state in the twentieth century. They also have been a long-time participant in anarchist and queer organizing spaces:

The older people I have been able to speak to who participated in the beginnings of the gay movement of the '70s unanimously shared that they joined other struggles precisely due to the oppression they experienced for their sexual orientation or gender identity. Probably, a hundred years ago, the great number of sexual dissidents we can find in the anticapitalist struggle, especially within anarchism, also felt called to the struggle for similar reasons.

The gentle sexual demands that fags, dykes, and transvestites began to spread during the Second Republic

(1931–1939), some coming from Marxism but especially from anarchism, were cut short by the Civil War, exile, World War II, and the climate of repression and authoritarianism that the Communist Party and Stalinism imposed within the workers' movement from the beginning of the Civil War. Here we encounter our first rupture in the continuity of memory, which Francoism turned into an even wider breach in the '40s, erasing both queer memory and that of the entire anticapitalist and workers' struggle.

Piro goes on to reveal how the loss of memory generates further losses. It pushes people towards reformist or even right-wing positions, such as the ongoing TERF offensive and post-COVID "conspiranoia" (conspiracy theory thinking) increasingly present in the Left:

The gravest consequence that this rupture has had in the last 30–40 years can be found amongst the hundreds and hundreds of queer people coming into social movements and struggles in the Spanish state without having absolutely any idea of the huge quantity of people like us who came before. I myself began to organize politically in 2005, in the context of the legalization of gay marriage and the huge fascist and ultra-Catholic protests against it, and my *marica*[33] self was implicated in this,

33 *Marica*, a feminine variant of *maricón*, translates most closely to "faggot" in English. It is another example of a practice of queering that we can find in the movements of oppressed people across the world: taking a term that is intended to be derogatory, reclaiming it, using it as an in-group way of self-identifying, and fucking up anyone who tries to use it against you, thus stealing a weapon of oppression from the oppressors and turning it into a form of power-from-below.

but I was not at all present in the radical queer struggles that came immediately before me, in the '90s, or in the gay movement of the '70s. I had to learn about all that on my own, and the same thing has occurred with practically all the queer people who entered political organizations that were not specifically queer or LGTBI.

This situation has caused a good part of the LGTBI/queer community of the Kingdom of Spain to identify more with assimilationists, homo-nationalists, or reformists generally led by powerful institutions, since anticapitalist organizations did not give due attention to this topic in the present nor did they remember their past in the '70s. And that has generated a feeling for many of us of being politically orphaned.

A century ago there was a well defined complicity between Left and Right to destroy sexual dissidence. Now, sexual orientation itself is not attacked, but rather adjacent questions, like flamboyance, promiscuity, or misgendering trans people. There has been and there continues to be a problem within the Spanish Left of not acknowledging privilege, which causes problems for sexual and gender dissidents, women, racialized people, disabled and neurodivergent people, causing many to abandon their collectives after associated conflicts. I think this is a low-intensity way of erasing us from history, and if they ever get the opportunity, erasing us from the face of the earth.

Simple reform, the victory of one political party or another, will never be enough to safeguard our survival. And those who do not see the current situation as urgent because they themselves are not being targeted with annihilation need to wake up to the fact that it is never okay to sit idle when others are facing that threat. They need to realize that annihilation is at the very core of the system we are held captive by. Annihilation of difference and colonization of all the survivors is the foundation for our global society. In one way or another, *it happened everywhere and it is still happening*.

Zarahn Southon is a Ngāti Tūwharetoa artist, and an anticolonial educator and organizer, living in Aoteorea. In Te Kotahitanga o Ngāti Tūwharetoa,[34] he is the delegate for Ngāti Kurauia. He wrote to me about the direct relationship between colonization, economic and cultural oppression, and the loss of memory; and the relationship between the decision to resist, the recovery of memory, and the expansion of a people's ability to fight back for their survival:

> Due to the impacts of the New Zealand Wars, the proletarianization of Māori and colonial assimilation well into the twentieth century, many of our tribal groups became fragmented. Tribal elders encouraged many young Māori to leave the rural life of our marae seeking opportunities in the cities. My parents were part of the urban drift in the 1970s. Despite the fragmentation we returned to the marae since our elders were ahi kaa (keeping the fires at home). They encouraged us to balance Te Ao Pākehā (the world of Europeans) with Te Ao Māori (the world of Māori). Despite the loss of the language among my parents' generation, the 773 marae Māori either newly built, restored, or conserved throughout the country have become a vital component of the broader pan-Māori movement revitalization effort and resistance to the state. [...]

---

34 Within the independence or unity movement, this is a reference to the Tūwharetoa people of the Māori, who are a confederation or unified group of many different peoples or nations. The Māori are occupied by New Zealand, a settler state established by the British.

Marae consist of a communal building called a wharenui (large meeting house), a marae atea (open space in front of meeting house), a whare kai (eating house), and in some cases a whare karakia (prayer house or church). Each marae is distinct in its own way; the more traditional ones are magnificent and elaborately carved and painted, with large dining halls and facilities, to more modest, austere, intimate, like a small hall built in a rural paddock. They are sacred spaces for celebrations, wānanga (learning), tangi (funerals), hui (meetings), and hakaari (feasts) [...]

Through the impact of colonisation and the Tohunga Suppression Act 1907, many of our ancient traditions like Matariki (star reading) were nearly lost. Therefore, our elders made the decision to pass knowledge to a select few. Today, these tohunga (expert practitioners in, e.g., healing, navigation, carving, etc.) are vital in passing on tribal knowledge to the next generation.

This strategic battle for memory clashes sharply with movement practices in zones of whiteness, where forgetting is rarely questioned and both memory and elders are often treated like baggage.

We already looked at some of the triumphs of the Bash Back! convergence in September 2023: the power, the ability to corrupt, pervert, and otherwise transform space. But I would be remiss if I did not also mention the experience of an older queer friend who described it as a sad space for themself and others of their generation. It was sad because of a lack of connection with the younger queers, a general lack of interest on the part of the younger ones to include the elders or understand the struggles that preceded them.

This disinterest in the past can resound as loudly as the slamming of a door. The truth is, we need support just to be able to stay in motion over decades.

"Being in and among movements for years has given me some of the most rewarding and most traumatic experiences I can recall," William C. Anderson writes in the introduction to *The Nation on No Map*, in which he makes an explicit connection between our ability to learn in movement and the intergenerationality of that movement: "we grow through learning. However, I admit, sometimes I wish that I'd had people around to tell me or warn me about certain things I ultimately found out later."[35]

Piro, the queer historian, also underscores how learning histories of resistance from books is a poor substitute for learning directly from the survivors of our struggles:

> I think the historians like myself who, over the last 10–15 years, have been digging through our community's past and its connections with struggle, are the people who have enabled a transmission of memory from one generation to the next. I wish it had been done directly, by the people directly involved, but so many of them did not survive the AIDS crisis of the '80s and '90s, many have had complicated lives that have drastically reduced their life expectancy, and others have for a long time had serious economic and health difficulties that have prevented them from continuing in the struggle.

Sylvie Kashdan has been involved in a variety of social justice movements and activities since the early 1960s. She stresses the particular difficulty:

---

35   William C. Anderson, *The Nation on No Map*, Oakland, CA: AK Press, 2021, p.xxi.

[...] for anarchists to learn from written histories because academia and book publishing have generally been dominated by Marxists of all sorts. And they have tended to either leave out the role of anarchists, to portray individual and groups of anarchists who played major roles as simply leftists, or portray them unsympathetically. There are also several cases in which authors have written sympathetic books about anarchist projects, such as the Home Colony in Washington State, without thinking to consult local anarchists.

What kind of changes have been necessary to be able to stay active in the movement as one gets older, I ask. Sylvie responds:

Some people I know changed their emphasis from direct action social struggle to media or artistic involvement. Some, like me, put a lot of emphasis on teaching and learning in anarchistic egalitarian contexts.

It gives me hope that nowadays there are more older people, proportionately, involved in anarchist/anti-authoritarian groups and activities than in the 1960s, 1970s, and much of the 1980s. But there should be more celebrations and other activities that are consciously focused on intergenerational participation. For example, a variety of protest music from different eras could be included. Maybe even some get-acquainted activities, such as people being asked to write a few sentences about themselves, and then what they have written is passed to a facilitator who reads them aloud and the group tries to guess who wrote those sentences (such as: "a famous honcho told me to get him a cup of coffee, but I refused ... ").

I have always thought that intergenerational cooperation is very important, and I sought out older people when I was young, to try working with them, but I didn't become a follower of any of them. And I hope that currently younger people are able to think of relations between the younger and older in terms of equality. But it often seems to be something that older anarchists and anti-authoritarians want more than younger people.

What Sylvie says reminds me of one of my conversations with Mertxe, a friend from the working-class Barcelona neighborhood of Pla de Besós. She has been a social movement participant in Catalunya since the early '90s. She's also a flamenco singer, and taught me much of what I know about squatting:

I have found that amongst the younger generations there are people (not everyone) who don't really want to fill themselves with the history of the social movements. They might want you to tell the occasional story, to hear about the little battles of the past, but nothing beyond a nice memento and a good while chatting. As though relating history weighed down the memory too much, and some *compas* who have more recently joined us need to free themselves from excess weight. As though, in order to feel like a part of the social movements, they want to create their own history, and to do so they have to show a lack of interest in earlier practices.

To a lesser extent, I notice some people are barely interested in making intergenerational connections but at the same time they don't cut off that contact with older *compas*, just in case they can profit off it somehow; people with a "we are in the present, we are the present generation, we dominate the present, and that is the basis for our actions" kind of energy.

On the other hand, it also happens that in some collectives, squatted social centers, houses, and projects that have been functioning for decades, they close up, they don't leave any space, and they don't open themselves up to the kinds of contributions fresh participants can offer. And in the face of youthful proposals, the "legends" (alternately, the "dinosaurs") respond in a discouraging way: *no, we've always done things this way*, or, *no, we tried that and it didn't work*. Words that land like a condemnation.

I would add that specifically the period of struggles from 1996–2004 which we so often bring up is engraved in our youth, for many of us. We flocked to the anarchist social centers, to some surviving neighborhood assemblies, and an entire inheritance of practices was conveyed to us from the antimilitarist collectives and the conscientious objectors [two major movements from the '70s and '80s]. We drew reflections from those experiences that served us in our struggles at that moment and in the future.

Mertxe then points out how the organizations that have most changed the landscape in Catalunya, in particular those enabling lower-class people to gain resources for survival and direct access to housing, "are an inheritance of" earlier groups created from within the anarchist and autonomous movement in the '90s and '00s. However, most participants in the recent wave of organizing are unaware of these earlier experiences, or they repudiate them on a simplistic level, which prevents them from learning anything:

I think that the strategies that we used a long time ago don't necessarily have to work now, but being familiar with them can help construct a narrative of the past, that we carry with us in the present, from which we can gather experiences for our struggles today and our struggles tomorrow.

Tasos Sagris, from Athens, has been in the streets for nearly four decades. He is a part of Void Network, an anarchist cultural community. We worked together on the book, *We Are an Image from the Future*, about the insurrection that spread across Greece in 2008. For the present book, I reached out to him to ask why our movements so often have to start from scratch, or start from zero, in the idiom we were using:

We don't start from zero, because then no one would become an anarchist. We wouldn't even have the memory of what it means to be an anarchist. Yet the memory exists. The inspiration exists. The infrastructure exists.

If we speak about the memory, memory comes from narration. The movements play this role of telling our stories. And the role of public spaces is to sustain the collective memory.

The big historical squats like Villa Amalais, Empros, and Lelas, these spaces, they sustain the memory of struggles but also the memory of our creativity. So we need squares, meeting places, places where we've been meeting for many years, like fifty years, places where people know they can go and meet anarchists, like the Polytechnic [a university with several buildings occupied for movement use, from the end of the dictatorship until very recently] or Exarcheia Square. These are the places we have in Athens, similar to Haight and Ashbury in San

Francisco, which was the meeting place of the hippies for like thirty years. It was just a crossroads. A social space can be just a crossroads, a place where you can go and know that you will meet your own people.

As for inspiration, it comes from our actions, it comes from our activity. For sure, you need to sustain activities. There is an element of appearance and disappearance, of growing and shrinking, moving with this rhythm is an important practice for us, but the memory needs to sustain our activities. For example, you need to celebrate days of memory on the anniversaries of important historical moments for the movement. Through this practice you weave a web of activities that somehow give us inspiration. The role of memory is to give inspiration, or otherwise it's just sadness. Always it's sadness because we are lost. We have been defeated, many times. But to not feel pathetic, to not just stay trapped in our legacy looking like we are nothing but an old thing, we have to inspire ourselves with action.

It's not always a bad thing to start from zero because then we feel young and fresh, we don't have to care so much about our legacy. I'm making a distinction between legacy and memory. Memory is to take inspiration from the past, it gives us a power to change the future. But legacy in the end is just sadness because the past is already gone, the past is already dead.

The problem with the anarchists is that we don't have sustained infrastructure. This is also because of State attacks, so we lose the occupied buildings, we will lose the squares, we will lose the places we meet. So all the time we have to be flexible, we have to be able to take new spaces. We have to move beyond the ability of the State to understand us, because when the State understands us, we lose the battle. So we don't have infrastructures that survive for many many years. It's difficult to have an example of anything that we've sustained for a hundred years, but the bourgeoisie, they have that. Their parliaments, their museums, their monuments, that's how they legitimize themselves, by showing that they've existed for hundreds of years, and they also do that by destroying our spaces to show that they are the only ones who last.

Yet we cannot use the attacks of the State as an excuse for not having sustained infrastructures. There's another problem, there.

I was reading this history of anarcho-communism, a huge, thick book. And every three pages, there is mention of another anarchist organization, a new organization that the anarcho-communists had formed. And just one page later, or one paragraph even, the organization ends. They never last more than three years, five years. We lose our spaces because of State attacks, but our organizations are not falling apart from State attacks usually, they are falling apart because of our own problems. The State destroys our spaces, but our organizations and our assemblies we destroy ourselves. And in our histories we don't explain why.

We need a specifically anarchist solution to this.

The Leftists have a solution to this problem that works for them. Leninism has a solution for this problem. The Communist Party of Greece was created in 1910, it has been existing for 110 years! Of course, they have been destroying the possibilities of revolution for 110 years, but they can last! In this way, they are like the bourgeoisie.

So we need anarchist ways of solving this problem, because we cannot use their ways. We need a way to sustain our organization or sustain our assemblies.

Tasos presents us with the theme of adaptability. It's okay if we are not permanent, especially considering the lengths the State will go to to destroy anything we build, uproot anything we plant. But we need to be honest with ourselves when we are the ones destroying ourselves, poisoning our own soil, turning our backs on our own memories.

We can build a continuity of experiences from one generation to the next, even if we lose spaces and have to transition from one organization or initiative to the next. We are not Ozymandias. We do not believe in permanence, like the State does. And clearly, as Tasos points out, we have built this continuity to a certain extent, as demonstrated by the simple fact that our movements are still here, resisting. But also, there is another question we are avoiding: why do we so easily become our own worst enemy? Why do we so often tear apart our own projects? To develop an adequate answer, we need to begin to plumb the depths of all the ways that capitalism, patriarchy, and white supremacy train us to reproduce alienation and harm.

Angustia Celeste is an anarchist and a friend who I can best describe as an inspiring balance of hellraiser and caretaker. They've been in the movement for about the same time as I have, and in many of the same countries. Needless to say, when I came with questions, they were already stewing with answers:

Honestly, it is fine to "drop out" or "take distance" from movements that do not meet needs in your life. We have a lifetime to engage and all those things that used to be framed as dropping out—like focusing on paid labor, building up stability, studying, raising children, slowly planning, and plotting but not immediately acting—those things are not dropping out anyway. Lay your foundation, work slowly toward future goals, allow yourself to determine your own needs, focus on your material world even if it takes you away from collective work for a while. Get individual therapy if it helps, take trips into nature, and get away from the city if you can. You do not have to be in the thick of it all the time. Hell, dealing with accumulated trauma *is* the thick of it sometimes.

Healing cannot be accomplished in isolation, but we are allowed to prune down and build up our communities and social relationships so they serve us. The feminization of care work and radical identity which requires that we engage in community labor, often backs people into a corner. Just because you have a skill, resource, just because there is a hurt, pain, a need, someone requesting care does not mean you have to meet those needs.

I asked them what they saw, in their experience, as vital factors that either allow people to sustain themselves in struggle over time, or prevent them from doing so:

Personally, I find the concept of cumulative moral injury to be very helpful. I do not feel acutely affected by any singular traumatic experience that has occurred, especially in settings where I have a purposeful role. Whether in the emergency room or out in the field doing humanitarian aid work, experiencing secondary trauma is something I have been able to manage when I can hold to the meaningful positive interventions I can offer, however small. But over time I have experienced burn out when resources, both physical and mental, have been outpaced by need. I struggle with scenarios where not only can I not alleviate or meaningfully mitigate harm, but I am actively participating in it. This happened to me in the context of the COVID-19 pandemic working in the ER and the ICU. I have also experienced exhaustion in relation to government repression, because it takes you away from your work and requires a lot of time and resources be spent doing essential, but reactive, legal support.

To be active over the course of decades, I have had to divest myself of the feeling of urgency that solidarity and care work carry. It is important to determine my engagement not by absolute need which knows no bounds, but by my capacity to do the work. The pandemic tested my commitment to this strategy, but you cannot study the sympathetic and parasympathetic response to stress and somehow exclude your own body from that equation.

I have cared for and watched so many people die over the last few years. I discovered I am not immune to the slow bleed that occurs with one moral injury after another. When the systems I was participating in relentlessly churned onward, expecting more while offering less and less resources, I found my ability to be a compassionate little cog diminish. I was pressed to my maximum capacity, and in greater isolation than ever before. We are not, however, alone in our grief.

Having a collective understanding of harm/trauma and contextualizing mental health crisis to a wider societal context provides an escape from the overwhelming isolation of depression/burnout. *Sociodiagnostics* (Frantz Fanon, 1967) clearly identifies colonialism itself as the pathological agent. We cannot divorce the symptoms from the wider causal agents. But this wider analysis does not necessarily offer up easy next steps. It is not a sign of health to be well adjusted to a profoundly sick society, definitively—but neither is it healthy to overly identify with dis-ease and the maladaptive coping mechanisms which spring from that despair. We exist within structures that do not offer respite or the resources or time for things beyond base survival. The work we do is dispiriting and wounding much of the time. How do we make room for healing? Sometimes healing requires radical changes to the pace of our work.

I worked more than full time in the emergency room well into my third trimester. Then I went into labor, and only then did I stop. I changed course, moved away, got therapy, quit critical care, refocused, stepped back, sank down, and turned inward. After parental leave ended, I got an easier job running a pediatric clinic in a homeless shelter, and took a break from direct aid.

Now that I am raising a toddler again, as a solo parent this time, it has remade my relationship to time, capacity, nourishment, and sleep. A new baby helped me take a careful survey of my social relationships—and prune those that did not feel supportive and generative. The realities of my work life are set by external dictums like capitalism, debt, and the not always straightforward delineation between a need and a desire, but I am trying to slow down. I am also trying to be realistic about my own needs as a caretaker.

I think people who identify heavily with the political work they do struggle to take periods of time for rest. I cannot sustain the level of trauma stewardship I used to. So, I try to extend to myself the graciousness I encourage my friends and comrades to have for themselves. We cannot hold responsibility for all the world's atrocities, and we cannot always redress all the harm that we are surrounded by. If you value your capacity for empathy and by extension your capacity for resistance, then you will make space for healing.

The sense of urgency we often feel can turn into something much more sustainable if we realize that this struggle goes beyond any one lifetime, that we are alive after we are dead because we live on in those who remember us. To quote a common saying from the Mapuche struggle: "We have been struggling for over 500 years. We may have to struggle 500 more, but we will win."

Speaking about George Floyd Square, Arianna Nason gives us an example of how we can protect ourselves from loss, from forgetting, when we orient our liberated spaces towards memory and when we fight to defend those spaces:

Memory and then healing are the main focuses of the Square. In that order. Every single item that is physically left at the Square is treated as an offering, a gift, a prayer, and it's preserved in an archive project. That's run by a nonprofit started by Jeanelle Austin, one of our neighbors. She's from a big family that goes way back in the neighborhood. Jeanelle runs the memory project, her sister Jeanette runs the medical services, and their brother Butchy leads a brass line band that goes to events.

Jeanelle just started taking care of offerings at the site and then it became something more official. It needed a lot of support, and the support flooded in. It would have been really different if the Minnesota Historical Society had come in. It would have looked really different because they have their lenses that they use, they have their stakeholders whispering in their ear about how it should be done. But the Austins are our neighbors, they're our cousins, and they've been a part of the neighborhood a lot longer than many of us. They were out there on Day One with all of us, offering prayer, offering hugs, offering music, holding space.

We are super-aggressive about holding down the space, we commit everything there, we hold memory in that space. We have lost community members, and we have put up murals of them or some type of symbolism or imagery of them up on our memorial wall, so they have a place to go to, so they always have a place to find the ones they've lost. It's important to do that in a way that's public and present. It's important to have a place where we are remembered.

Every offering is a gift, every offering is a prayer, every offering contributes to us being able to hold onto what we've lost.

38th and Chicago is about George Floyd, it's about Black liberation, it's about liberation from police and police violence, but it's become about so much more than that; it's become about giving a shit about each other, making sure that everyone's needs are met. We do not leave anyone behind. Every memory is valuable and every life is valuable, equally and the same.

When we liberate space, when we intentionally transform that space, and when we fight to defend it, to keep it alive, the possibilities for transformation that unfold before us start to become limitless. And when we have something important to fight for, we have shown time and again that we are more powerful than the cops. When we defeat the cops, the State looks for other ways to destroy our liberated space, to destroy its spirit when they cannot destroy it physically. Which should teach us that the victory is never the legalization of our hard-won infrastructures, it is opening up that process of transformation itself and following where it takes us.

What does the spiritual destruction of a liberated place look like? It can be accomplished through a thousand mechanisms, all of which might be referred to as "pacification." Making it conform to a preexisting architectural model, like a park or a school; taming it to fit within a single-issue focus; turning it into a museum; gentrifying the area so only the wealthy can access it.

Speaking about gentrification, Arianna tells us, "The memory isn't gone but the people who hold them have had to leave that spot." That nuance—not a loss of memory but a *displacement* of memory—begs us to consider the question of diasporas, especially considering how integral displacement is both to colonialism and to racial capitalism. Cindy Milstein is a Jewish anarchist who captures beautifully the dual nature of diaspora: "Diaspora has always been bound up with wrenching hardship and yet, inextricably, tantalizing promise." They explain the Greek roots of the word, meaning to sow in all directions, and quote a Greek anarchist friend:

I think of diaspora as the spreading of seeds across both space and time. It is a scattering apart, and also a seeding of many places and moments. It holds pain, loss, and separation, but hope, growth, and nurturance too.[36]

Celeste again:

People tend to get involved in social movements when they are young and have a different relationship to nurturing. As you age, you need to reassess and revisit capacity to not totally run yourself into the ground. If you were sustained in your work when you were younger

36 Cindy Milstein, *There Is Nothing So Whole As a Broken Heart: Mending the World As Jewish Anarchists*, AK Press, 2021, p.xvi. Milstein quotes paparouna, pp. xvi–xvii.

by older friends and comrades who contributed wisdom and resources and less in time and action, consider this might someday apply to you! Also imagine a community realm where changes in engagement are understood as necessary, instead of judged. Most people who tell me stories of cutting ties and reducing engagement are really telling me a story about a changing need they had in their life that their community could not accommodate.

The attempt is the achievement. It is the process itself that is sustaining and is itself the vital factor. When you create spaces that allow you to reflect, sleep, plan, play and nurture yourself, your children, your friendships, it allows you to do political work over the span of decades. The only gem of advice I can offer is that it is OK to do less, with more intention, as you age.

There are many ways to engage, many of them small and unacknowledged by a political community that is still bad at recognizing daily care work. I think of all my friends who never got to the space of collective resistance because they lost the battle within themselves first, and I am reminded by their absence that this work of healing, loving, and nurturing is front-line work. Survival is resistance, but to quote Leonard Cohen, why not ask for more?

Care in Conflict

The State engineers systems that incapacitate us. It imposes dependency, encloses the commons, poisons our bodies, multiplies hierarchies, encourages obedience and betrayal, and creates scarcity, while spreading a self-destructive culture. All that harm has to go somewhere, and the probable outcome is that people turn to self-defeating behaviors, or they harm others at the same level or on lower levels of the social hierarchy. The violence of oppression filters outwards and downwards.

The same State that produces class and race then criminalizes racialized groups and lower-class culture, locking up people who need healing and resources. The whole cycle of crime and punishment can destroy communities and rip up neighborhoods. And it is no coincidence that communities and subcultures that become famous for their resistance in one generation are immersed in various forms of self-harm by the next generation, leading to the loss or distortion of memories of rebellion.

Sometimes we lose people to drugs. Addiction and overdose are disproportionately experienced by people with trauma, people outside our society's unhealthy norm for mental health, people in poverty, and people from colonized and racialized communities. Lorenzo Kom'boa Ervin describes the flooding of specifically Black communities with dangerous drugs as "chemical warfare [that is] used to destabilize our communities and keep us from fighting back."[37]

When the State criminalizes drugs, it suppresses the spiritual traditions of colonized cultures, denies people's right to experiment or self-medicate, and erases the science around effective responses to addiction. Drugs become simply an excuse to wage literal war against poor and racialized neighborhoods. And by the logic of the market, criminalization raises drugs' value, turning them into a fuel for the gang wars that devastate lower-class and racialized neighborhoods.

37   Lorenzo Kom'boa Ervin, *Anarchism and the Black Revolution*, London: PM Press, 2021, p.119.

The story of gangs is also more complex. They have been an organizing force in many of the anti-police rebellions of recent years. Gangs are often the most agile and dedicated structures to respond forcefully to racist violence, when all of the big organizations that supposedly represent oppressed communities are calling for nonviolence and patience. They can be mechanisms for surviving in a war zone, and often what get described as gangs are just friendship groups of lower-class and racialized young people.

Black revolutionaries from Fred Hampton to Lorenzo Kom'boa Ervin have promoted organizing with gang members in a way that addresses the contradictions of criminalized resistance and culture. They've also criticized how gangs frequently reproduce poor-on-poor and Black-on-Black harm while making it easier for the State to justify its brutal policing of racialized neighborhoods. Ervin writes: "The present internal crisis is the result of an environment where poverty rules, drugs and violence (both social and physical) are rampant and life is sometimes considered cheap. It is undeniable that crimes and other internal violence are destroying our community."[38]

William C. Anderson approaches the question by centering the need for Black people "to defend ourselves in the war that is already happening all around us and in the wars that are to come." Necessary considerations of self-defense must include gangs, both for the capacities they offer and the forms of harm they help perpetuate:

Those who are most familiar with fighting in the streets are needed too, which will require people to look beyond the trauma and the stigma of "criminality."

38   Ervin, *Anarchism*, p.146.

Such transformations should recognize and center the experiences of the women, children, sex workers, and other community members who have borne the brunt of violence. This means we must also address how regularly they must protect themselves from the likes of gangs and the militaristic, patriarchal violence that creates constant clashes. Like the gangs, they know how to fight and resist and defend themselves in ways many of us can learn from.[39]

As an adaption to racist dispossession and urbanization, gang structures are entangled with the culture of hip-hop. After the obliteration of the Civil Rights Movement, hip-hop existed on the cusp between memory and forgetting, subversion and commodification, all while being criminalized by broader society. Hip-hop scholar Austin McCoy hones in on patriarchal violence embedded in hip-hop culture, while also acknowledging its subversive stance, for example, how a hip-hop artist can talk about the revolution "as a statement mocking the lost promise of the Civil Rights Movement":

When RZA told listeners, "Yo Shorty, you don't even gotta go to summer school. / Pick up the Wu-Tang double CD and you'll get all the education you need this year," I took his word for it. Or at least I wanted to, because there was nothing else to believe in. [...]
    I saw myself as part of a beleaguered imaginary community, or a "hip-hop nation." The killings of Shakur and Biggie Smalls threw the culture into a crisis. Violence had snatched the genre's two most promising artists.

39 Anderson, *The Nation on No Map*, pp.132, 136.

> Who was next? Where was hip-hop going? Where was
> I going?[40]

The fact that tools of resistance can also reproduce patterns of harm illustrates an important lesson: struggle is messy. People who come in looking for a pure path to revolution either end up learning, or they gravitate to some self-destructive sect that promises easy answers.

Good and Evil are concepts of the colonizers. There is no binary moral scale that can give us the complexity and the compassion we need in order to heal and create something truly different, because in any system, a thing and its opposite contain the same logic: they reproduce each other, they recall each other. And none of us are pure because all of us have been enlisted to help reproduce this oppressive system just to survive.

The struggle for transformative justice comes out of this historical fight against prison and police, while also surviving patriarchal and poor-on-poor violence. It is a struggle for survival and also a struggle for healing and compassion. Not compassion for the police—that is an institution that is oppressive to its very core. But centuries of being policed have affected all of us in different ways, and those are wounds that still need healing. Long-time Black feminists Mariame Kaba and Andrea Ritchie write how:

> Our organizing and advocacy toward a world free of
> policing is rooted in the reality that, for many of us, the
> cops offer no solution to violence, and in fact *are* the
> killers, rapists, home invaders and looters, destroyers of

---

40   Austin McCoy, "It's Bigger Than Hip-Hop," *The Baffler*, no. 72, January 2024.

lives, families, and communities. *They* are what stands between us and the resources we need to ensure our collective safety and survival.

If we are to have any hope, we need to see how self-defense, survival, healing, and compassion actually require the same kind of transformations from us. A huge part of the harm that cycles between people and filters downwards in our society is produced and reproduced by white supremacy, patriarchy, capitalism, and ableism. But at no moment are any of these systems of oppression separate: they are fully entangled, they reproduce one another, and at least in their current configurations all across the globe, none of them could exist independently of the others:

> We need to hold our communities' fears with care while simultaneously building a shared understanding of violence and harm that includes the violence of police and fellow community members, of how we might go about creating genuine safety together, in ways that recognize the interconnectedness of our existence, without leaving anyone behind.[41]

Kaba and Ritchie recount an antiracist gathering in Cleveland in the wake of the Ferguson uprising, how a group of participants came across the police trying to arrest a young Black boy, how they held their ground, surrounded the police, and unarrested him, all while keeping one another safe:

---

41   This and the previous block quote are both from Mariame Kaba and Andrea Ritchie, "Reclaiming Safety," *Inquest*, August 30, 2022.

> While initially the target of police action was a Black boy,
> we recognized, responded to, and resisted all forms of
> violence against all Black people the incident involved.
> And we were led, in large part, by Black women, queer
> and trans people. Our collective response represented
> Black feminism in action: Black feminism offers a vision
> for liberation not just for Black women, but for our entire
> community, and for all who experience oppression.
>
> We are Black feminist abolitionists. This means we are
> shaped by Black feminism and abolition feminism—and
> their intersections.[42]

The needs they express to create genuine safety and not leave anyone behind are erased by the practice that has gained the most mainstream visibility, which is a sort of middle-class comfort politics. This practice evades identification and criticism because sometimes it coopts the language of transformative justice, while at other times it mischaracterizes and rejects it. We can recognize it by naming what it centers: ultimatums, public call-outs, subcultural scenes and in-groups, ostracism, timelines for healing decided from above, failure to create a continuum of action from major institutions to harmful individuals, and little actual support for people who have been hurt. Despite its blustery rhetoric and high tolerance for cruelty, this practice doesn't actually build any capacity to deal with broader forms of social violence or people who don't follow the in-group's codes.[43]

---

42 Mariame Kaba and Andrea J. Ritchie, "How Abolition Feminism Fuels the Movement for Black Liberation," *Lit Hub*, September 1, 2022.

43 Much of the critique I'm referencing happens in support circles, mediation processes, and gatherings that don't end up publishing any texts to avoid airing painful and activating stories; however,

The practitioners of this comfort politics would have been unable to protect me from the people who hurt me when I was a child: it's probably no coincidence that they habitually ignore people outside a certain age range. They are suspiciously silent on questions of racist harm, and time and again we have seen them either use or silence people who are surviving gendered violence, without offering any actual support or resources for healing.

This method for dealing with the immense problem of harmful and abusive behaviors that are present in all of our circles is not only inadequate, it makes the problem worse. And it should set off alarm bells how much this practice is encouraged and accelerated by the alienated, toxic spaces of social media.

I know how satisfying it can feel to use what is in truth a punitive, superficial practice and in hindsight I can see that when I did, I made our movement an unhealthier place, and I made myself an unhealthier person.

I might not be amongst a majority of anarchists when I say there is a place for vengeance in liberation movements; when we strike back against a more powerful enemy, we change the power dynamics, and that kind of proactive movement can also help trauma move through our bodies. However, when we harm someone who is less powerful than us, we are reinforcing the logic of states and making ourselves less able to deal with conflict or harm in an abolitionist, anarchist way.

Vengeance should not occupy a major role in liberation movements. Though the ability to attack is vital, it's the solidarity at the heart of collective self-defense, as well as mutual

there are exceptions. One text from London that names these patterns is Fourth Wave: London Feminist Activists, "When Abusers Hijack the Language of Feminism," *Freedom News*, September 2018.

aid, reciprocity, and an emphasis on healing and reconcilia-
tion that make the foundations for a healthy, free, stateless
society. A deeper plunge into history teaches us that vengeance uncodified leads to war between neighbors, whereas
codified vengeance is the origin of punitive law.

And though the practitioners of a superficial response to
harm generally tell themselves they are punching upwards and
fighting against oppressive hierarchies, the ease with which
we can ostracize people today—how the power dynamics and
the architecture of social media and society today are actually
on our side when we try to cancel people from our scenes, how
easy it is to knock people down even while the millionaires,
the police, and the politicians retain absolute impunity—just
goes to show this is an obvious fiction. We need to be more
self-reflective than this.

It is easy and understandable to feel some joy when someone
who has abused people left and right is punished or made to
suffer. This joy, however, is a reaction to life in a prison society;
it is not the seed that grows into a healthier world. Speaking
to how many online abolitionists celebrated the news that
R. Kelley was finally going to prison after inflicting sexual
violence on fans for years, Mariame Kaba and Rachel Herzing
empathized, but stated unequivocally:

> Mistaking emotional satisfaction for justice is also not
> abolitionist [...] abolition is not about your fucking
> feelings. Of course, everything involves feelings, but
> celebrating anyone's incarceration is counter to [Prison
> Industrial Complex] abolition.
>
> This may frustrate or anger people who want to claim
> an abolitionist identity or politic despite not being ready
> to operate from basic abolitionist principles. We under-
> stand. For years, both of us have facilitated community

accountability processes to address interpersonal harms (particularly involving sexual and intimate partner violence). As survivors of sexual harm, accountability is always at the forefront in our consciousness. We understand how damaging and serious sexual violence is. And we too have sometimes wished that abolition wasn't so rigorous in its demands of our politics.[44]

Favoring ostracism over change and healing can loop right back around into the prison system, given how ostracism lies at the heart of a carceral logic. Jenny, the abolitionist and prison solidarity organizer, had this to share:

People who come out of prison are ... people. They are not infallible. They make mistakes. Sometimes big ones. And our expectations of them are set impossibly high. It's like we set them up to fail. And then when they inevitably do, it's like a feeding frenzy to see who can do the most damage the fastest. It's devastating.

Radical movements so often seem to have two contradictory understandings of perfection. There is widespread condemnation of it as an ideal, or even as a possibility. But when it comes down to the real world and real people making real mistakes, there is no room for anything but perfection. We destroy ourselves and each other when we move from this place. This is one reason why so many people leave movements. We all seek a place where we can be held and cared for as full-blown humans with all of our complexities and faults without being torn asunder every time we make a

44 Mariame Kaba, *We Do This 'Til We Free Us: Abolitionist Organizing and Transforming Justice*, Chicago, IL: Haymarket Books, 2021, p.133.

mistake. People aren't running from accountability. They are running from annihilation. And so often these things happen when people are at their most vulnerable—for example, when they are coming out of prison. When they need care and support and, yes, help reacclimating to what it means to be a human in the free(er) world. People leaving prison after spending years locked in a cage have often had to fight so fiercely just to maintain their day-to-day humanity. It is outrageous to ever expect anyone to be perfect, but especially after this.

If we want people to continue being a part of communities of resistance we need to stop actively pushing them away. We need to care for each other even when we make mistakes. We need to find better ways of handling conflict, ways that draw people towards us instead of scaring them away. As a long-time prison abolitionist, I have to believe that people can heal. That they can do better. And that applies with just as much force to my friends as it does to all of the strangers I have fought for. Making a mistake doesn't make us a bad person, it just makes us human. We say things like this when we talk about prisons all the time. So why is it any different when we are talking about our friends and comrades?

There are so many in our movement who are amazing healers, amazing mediators, amazing support people, and amazing teachers, many of them drawing on multiple generations of learning and experience. If our movements are to be places of long-term survival and resilience, places that make us better people, we need to value and center the work they do.

Lessons Lived

We have overthrown states going back 4,000 years.[45] Anti-state rebellions in Africa and societies that organized themselves to oppose domination internal and external were a bulwark of resistance to the international slave trade. At the time the Invasion began in 1492, the majority of the Americas were stateless. Earlier revolutions or transformations towards proactively decentralized, reciprocal societies had changed the social landscape from the Amazon to the Andes, and from the Mississippi River Valley and Appalachia to the Colorado Plateau. That wealth of knowledge around decentralized organizing and communal, relational worldviews still informs movements today. Even the lower classes of Europe, after being subjected to hundreds or thousands of years of state authority, held on to traditions of commoning and resistance that shaped early anticapitalist movements.

If we look, if we listen, we will find a wealth of experiential knowledge all around us. One thing that shines out right away is that after 4,000 years, no matter how powerful oppressive systems have become, they still have not been able to defeat our struggles for freedom. Ricard de Vargas, the Catalan anarchist who grew up under the Francoist dictatorship and is still in struggle sixty years later, expresses it this way:

> The struggles for our individual and collective emancipation never end. They begin and end and always find continuity in multiple spaces in our colonized lives. For a revolutionary, for an anarchist, there are no defeats:

---

45 For more on the formation of early states and the many rebellions against them, see my book, *Worshiping Power: An Anarchist View of Early State Formation*, AK Press, 2017.

there are always tasks to carry out so we can continue
growing through our experiences, our wins and losses.

While we may never actually lose, *feeling* defeated is often
enough to break us. And while we may never actually lose
those who struggle alongside us, *thinking* that we've lost them
may be enough to sever the relationship, to sever the possibility of learning from one another.

How do we protect ourselves from loss when the whole of
this society is designed to erase us, pacify us, and enlist us to
do its dirty work, all at once?

I believe the answer is that there are no finished answers,
that we need to spend our entire lives learning and growing,
that in fact a fundamental aspect of freedom is that it is not
a perfected state we arrive in, but an undefined path we are
allowed to explore, a spaciousness that allows us to change and
move together.

Memory must not become a museum. As Mertxe shared
with me, "history also obstructs memory if it is not a conversation with room for many voices." She was referring to
how the anticapitalist movement in Barcelona had granted
myth-like status to a major battle her neighbors had fought
against the city government in 1990. But in the retelling, they
omitted the use of racist accusations against *gitano* neighbors,
accusing city planners of stabbing *white* residents in the back
while favoring *gitanos* who were actually much more marginalized. By sanitizing the story, white anticapitalists reinforced
a movement culture that further excluded people of color, and
they denied themselves the chance to improve their practices
of antiracist solidarity.

If our own movement histories help repackage defeats as
victories, we lose the ability to understand how the State
defeats us and we mistake institutions that have betrayed us

repeatedly for potential allies. Ricard de Vargas explains how the Spanish transition from a forty-year fascist dictatorship to a democracy, led by the Socialist Party, was really a pact between "the institutions governed by the political heirs of Franco and the leftwing parties that struck a deal" with them:

> The institutional Left played a clearly negative role in terms of the recovery of historical memory. They always tried to hide, minimize, or even falsify the revolutionary side of this memory, given how it hurt their Party and the interests of power. They've all wanted to erase any memory of the revolutionary anarchist conquests in the war, like the collectivizations of workers and peasants, or later experiences like the anarchist and anti-Francoist *guerrilla* in Catalunya that resisted for over twenty years in struggle, with around a thousand fighters killed in combat. And subsequently the political parties of the current system have made an intensive effort to treat groups and figures like the MIL [Iberian Liberation Movement] or Puig Antich as simply anti-Francoist movements, forgetting about their anticapitalist practice and their emphasis on social transformation. That's why the recovery of an anarchist historical memory has been carried out over all these years by diverse collectives opposed to the official history.

This suppression of memory by the institutional Left is even more significant, given how it erases a specifically anarchist history of armed struggle. Even that term, *"armed struggle,"* recalls a series of Marxist-Leninist, vanguardist groups like the MIR, RAF, the Weather Underground, Red Brigades, ETA, each with their logos and acronyms. What has been deliberately left out of the account is how, to a significant extent, they got their mode of struggle, techniques for picking locks, establishing safe houses, robbing banks, and forging passports—and in some cases, their very first weapons—from clandestine anarchists particularly active in Spain, Uruguay, Argentina, France, and the Balkans in the early and mid-twentieth century.

The difference is, the anarchist groups generally stayed anonymous because they saw their role as lending new capacities and sharper teeth to the struggle of the lower classes, rather than pretending to lead that struggle. But they faced the worst repression from the State, none of the attention from media and academics that was heaped on the vanguardists, and their erstwhile comrades on the Left helped erase even the memory of them.

Nestor Makhnovicki (a pseudonym) is an anarchist and antifascist who grew up in Poland at the end of Communist Party rule and through the transition to neoliberal democracy. Though the Polish government was less repressive than that of the USSR, there was still a tight control over the historical narrative:

State socialism tried to appropriate some of the movements that existed and then erased the memory of the others, or at least avoided mentioning them, if they could not be coopted for the ruling ideology. So for example, despite the fact of Poland having strong revolutionary traditions of socialist and anarchist movements, only the Communist resistance was ever really mentioned, or if the socialists were mentioned it was only the ones who could be coopted into the Party line. Uncomfortable passages would be omitted, and the memory would be manipulated for the Party's own needs.

When it comes to movement elders, people who lived through these struggles, there were some but not many. My grandfather was a Communist and he was in the armed resistance during the Second World War, and also involved in political organizing before the war, but I didn't really get to talk to him about these things while he was alive, I actually learned a lot more about him after he died.

Before 1990, libraries were free access but many materials that contradicted the official history weren't exactly there. After that, if you looked through different memoirs of the resistance in the Second World War, you could find a great deal of information, useful lessons on how to organize underground resistance movements, both armed resistance and political resistance, but they were scattered all over the place and you had to put significant effort into finding them and compiling them.

Only later some comrades managed to track down old members of the anarchist movement or their families, and started getting access to their memories and their diaries. So we gained that knowledge but at a later stage. You can always learn a great deal from history, I just wish we knew about these people when they were still alive and as it happened, we only managed to catch a few of them at the end of their lives.

With the transition to a neoliberal democracy, there was a period when there was really a lot of access to archives, but as the Polish government became more and more rightwing, they started a very intense policy of historical revisionism with a rightward bent, as opposed to the historical revisionism under the Communist regime, so basically the pendulum just went from one side to the other. Doing the same things, making some people into heroes of the resistance but never talking about the politics they had or even trying to falsely claim some people for the rightwing even though they were antifascists or leftwing activists.

When I emigrated, I met a lot of people who had been active in a lot of historical events in the anarchist movements of the past; it was a very interesting and new experience to be able to actually talk to people like that. Emigrating gave me that possibility, and for the first time made me realize the very possibility of multigenerational movements, because there were elders who were still active. It was very inspiring.

Laura Guillén Sahún knows that recovering memory is healing work, thanks to a great labor carried out by her mother, Maria Rosa. Maria Rosa grew up under the fascist dictatorship in Spain. She was taught that her maternal grandfather, executed in the Civil War, was a criminal and a bandit, and that her grandmother, who wasn't legally married, was a shamed woman. But she began to dig deeper when she saw that there was a heavier silence at work, keeping her own mother and father from speaking about the past. The spark came when she discovered, well into adulthood, that her father had been interned in a French concentration camp after fleeing political persecution in fascist Spain, and no one had ever told her about this growing up.

What Maria Rosa learned was both heartbreaking and inspiring. In fact, her grandparents, Josep Gardenyes and Maria Pont Colomines, were deeply in love and they were committed anarchists. Over the prior decades, they organized in the anarchist labor federation (the Confederación Nacional del Trabajo or CNT). Maria Pont helped organize the factory she worked in, and both of them participated in the armed struggle.

When a partial revolution broke out, led by those fighting a fascist coup attempt, they supported it fully. Josep continued to participate in actions, carrying out expropriations against the bourgeoisie to fund the struggle. A few weeks after the revolution broke out, though, he was caught, summarily executed, and thrown in an unmarked grave.

In the following decades, the dominant part of the anarchist movement refused to talk about this and similar acts of repression. Why? Because that dominant faction had pushed the CNT into the doomed strategy of putting the revolution on hold in order to support the antifascist government, which was controlled by the Socialists and then the Communists.

During this time, it was the Socialists and the Communists who carried out the majority of extrajudicial executions on the antifascist side, going primarily not after fascists but after anarchists and competing factions on the Left. But in the case of Maria Rosa's grandfather, it turned out it was the would-be leadership of the CNT who ordered and carried out the execution.

The repression of memory, the failure to acknowledge betrayals and mistakes, left scars that lasted for generations. Laura spoke with me about what this has meant in her own life, and for her family:

Since I first started becoming conscious of what family means, where we come from and what people make up my family tree, I began to ask questions about what the lives of my grandparents were like, and then my great grandparents. As an adolescent I was gripped by a need to dive into the history of my maternal great-grandparents, since I gradually came to see that their lives were completely tied up with the most important historical episode of recent times in our land: the Spanish Civil War and what went on immediately before and after it.

I gained a much clearer view of my values in life. For that reason, words like anarchism, labor struggles, the working class, feminism, and antifascism are words that define me. Gradually I came to have a deep admiration for my great-grandparents and the struggle of their era. [...]

It wasn't until my mother embarked on her research and we began to understand what really happened with her grandfather that I realized there was a hidden element to the story, even beyond the fact that anything referring to anarchism is already censored. It didn't appear in any book and even the closest social movements didn't talk about it.

That's when I understood that not everything is black and white, that there are a lot of contradictions even in social movements where it seemed clear which was the path to freedom.

Laura recounts how recovering the true history not only restored the dignity "of my great-grandparents as individuals," but it also helped to "make visible the collective struggle the anarchist movement carried out":

For me personally, my work is to pass on to my own kids (I have twins, 3 years old) all these values of struggle that our great-grandparents and grandparents taught us. I want to pass on a love for the people who came before us, esteem and admiration for them, to never forget what happened and never allow it to happen again.

My mother, in her moment, didn't have an easy time, because of the generation she was a part of, because she was a woman from the working class, but I absolutely admire her insistence and persistence in this project, and in her life in general. Thanks to just a few people, we have a path to follow, a line of inquiry to discover the truth, and little by little we'll achieve that new world in our hearts.

The official histories of dictatorships, and democracies, and authoritarian revolutions have more similarities than differences, because they are all erasures, an imposition of forgetting and silence The only way to make sure that an anarchist history does not become an act of silencing is to abolish the very concept of a singular objective history. Our histories are specific but entangled. Every community needs the power to narrate its own history, and every narration needs multiple voices, room for questions and disagreements. And between these different histories there also needs to be dialogue and critique.

Oppressed peoples in particular need to fight for their own histories to resist assimilation into the dominant history. William C. Anderson underscores this point in regards to Black anarchism:

Aside from Ervin, some other early and influential Black anarchists are Ashanti Alston, Kuwasi Balagoon, Martin Sostre, and Ojore Lutalo. These were revolutionaries who became disillusioned with things they saw happening in the Black Panther Party and Black movements they had been participating in. As Lutalo describes it: "In 1975 I became disillusioned with Marxism and became an anarchist (thanks to Kuwasi Balagoon) due to the inactiveness and ineffectiveness of Marxism in our communities along with repressive bureaucracy that comes with Marxism." So they turned away from Leninism, Stalinism, and Maoism toward the development of Black and New Afrikan anarchisms. This is something that distinguishes Black anarchism from classical anarchism. It is a split from within Black movements as opposed to simply being an effort to diversify or revise classical anarchism. White anarchists and others who herald the latter and defend the whiteness of anarchist movements by tokenizing Black anarchists highlight another dogmatic misstep. Black anarchism, of course, has much in common with classical anarchism, but it is Black-centered, specific to Black people and our unique conditions.[46]

Similarly, José Llanquileo, a Mapuche *werken* and former prisoner fighting for the liberation of Wallmapu, explains:

The Left consider the Mapuche as just another sector of the oppressed, an opinion we don't share. Our struggle is taking place in the context of the liberation of a people. Our people are distinct from Western society.

In the second half of the twentieth century, many Mapuche participated in Marxist movements that promised some form of national liberation, but failed to achieve their goals and left many Indigenous people feeling exploited, with the Mapuche being treated as "cannon fodder." Contrary to forced inclusion in a global working class whose experiences and needs are described in very eurocentric terms, Llanquileo asserts: "We

---

46 Anderson, *The Nation on No Map*, p.82. Anderson quotes Ojore Lutalo from the Anarchist Black Cross Federation website: www.abcf.net/.

are our own people, with our own history, and our struggle comes directly out of that."

Those of us who are white cannot theorize the resistance of racialized and Indigenous peoples nor write their histories, and it's not alright to paternalistically "leave a little room for it" and move on. But we can amplify it, challenge ourselves with it, support it, and learn what solidarity really means. I think it means understanding whose freedom is wrapped up with our own and risking ourselves to have their backs ... and every day finding ways to attack whiteness and colonialism within our own lives.

One thing any of us can pick up on, no matter who we are and where we're coming from, is a common theme in these experiences from earlier generations, from one side of the globe to the other: our own movements can recreate exactly what we are fighting against, whether in our day-to-day organizing or when our revolutions succeed and overthrow earlier power structures.

Sylvie Kashdan consistently emphasized how important it was for different generations to learn from one another in conversation, without dogmas or inflexible positions. But at the end of our interview, she also had one clear lesson she wanted to impart, something that has been confirmed again and again in all the struggles she has participated in over the last sixty years:

> While cooperation between people of different backgrounds and tendencies is of value, I think it is important for older anarchists to let younger people know about the dangers of attempts at cooperation between anarchists and anti-authoritarians on the one hand, and authoritarian leftists on the other. All too

often the latter have taken over projects when they had the chance.

What does it mean, then, if we reject total relativism but also reject dogma? What does it mean that after analyzing our own experiences and those of the people who came before us, we insist on drawing firm conclusions to guide our actions and strategies, but we also don't want anyone to take our conclusions as law?

What it means is that freedom is not a destination, but a way of getting there. It means each of us learning to find our paths, together and apart. Not all positions are valid, but the important thing is not being correct; it's learning how to draw lessons, how to recognize paths that manifest our freedom and the freedom of others, and how to recognize paths that actually build new prisons. Every new generation needs to develop this capacity for itself.

If we look at our histories of struggle, it's clear that we've made similar mistakes again and again, and that we need to be able to name those mistakes and pass them on as lessons. What is much less clear is what the best decision is in each historical moment. When we hone in on the details, we will probably notice that while the patterns of our mistakes resonate, it is more of a rhyme than a repetition; the particulars are always different. So while there are errors we should know by now to avoid, *there is still no blueprint for revolution, and there never will be, because everyone's needs are different, because every time and place has its unique characteristics, and because revolution means learning how to walk the path for ourselves.*

What I am offering below is exactly in this spirit: after the handful of years and rebellions I've lived through myself, after all the conversations I've had with revolutionary elders on five different continents, and after all the accounts of other friends and comrades I've sought out and listened to, I think we need to be confident about certain revolutionary assertions.

These are our lessons lived and our lessons learned. None of these, however, give us stable answers, for the reasons I just named. But how much more intelligent we are when we're in conversation with revolutionaries all around the world, when we can look at a thousand years of experience in the light of our present moment! If, on the contrary, we always have to start from scratch, we will probably never become astute and resilient enough to overcome the State.

Revolutionary movements that use authoritarian means carry the seeds of new states and new oppressions within them. They will damage our movements for liberation by suppressing disagreement and attacking those who do not agree with their blueprint and their methods, they will be absorbed by the states they fight against, or they will overthrow those states only to impose new configurations of oppression and exploitation. This is because **all states in history base their power on robbing us of our ability to organize our own lives. All states have been ecocidal, and all states have pursued warfare against their neighbors.**

Vanguardist groups always hold back the struggle. Their ideology tells them it is their role to "lead the masses." They end up confusing what is good for their organization with what is good for the revolution itself. Their actions are designed to capture the spotlight, monopolize the microphone, and spread their logo everywhere. Time and time again, vanguardist cults profit off of popular revolts to launch fundraisers that they spend on salaries and advertising for their own group, while people who actually made the revolt happen sit in jail, waiting for lawyers and bail funds.

And woe to anyone who runs out ahead of the vanguard: give anyone the idea that they're not actually leading things, and they will denounce you as a provocateur or a privileged adventurist, while working with the police to get you arrested.

You don't have to be a cop to do a cop's work. Police infiltrators in the '60s and '70s got many movements to destroy themselves by spreading false accusations that movement participants were snitches: this is called "snitch-jacketing" or "bad-jacketing." It turns out that discovering whether someone is actually a cop is less relevant than whether they act in a way that hurts the struggle.

A macho culture values danger over safety, and can encourage people to boast about things that should remain secret. A lack of emotional support in our circles increases the psychological damage we incur through our secrecy. At either end, a patriarchal culture puts us in danger of the isolation of prison or the loneliness of alienation.

Earlier movements had to learn the hard way that they were destroying themselves by ostracizing, beating up, or killing supposed snitches on the basis of a rumor or accusation. They made themselves stronger by improving their quality of communication, cracking down on rumors, and developing means to investigate and respond to the content of rumors, in the case of serious accusations. And they pushed for movements built around stronger interpersonal connections, which made them harder to infiltrate and made people less likely to snitch.

We need to recommit to similar efforts. Over the past few years, as new infiltrators are uncovered, we've had one opportunity after another to see how they turn the weaknesses of our movements to their advantage. So many of them got away with abusing and manipulating romantic partners within the movement. They have also used our practices of rumor-spreading and public accusations to cause internecine battles or prevent their discovery as undercovers.

It shouldn't be any surprise that we don't have examples of infiltrators who spent their time in the movement helping us develop better security practices, a healthier culture of communication and conflict resolution, or techniques for changing patriarchal behaviors. Police infiltrators have been abusers, and they have spread rumors of abuse, but what they won't do is help us build up responses based in transformative justice. Why? Because practices that truly end our dependence on a prison society also keep us safer from the police.

We need to identify and develop the practices that make us stronger no matter where the threat is coming from. We need to identify and spread the tools that allow us to support one another, to communicate safely and effectively, to heal from trauma, to defend ourselves, and to grow from conflict.

Reformism does not bring us the victories we think it does. Most reforms are just ways the system makes itself more efficient. Reforms that actually make our lives better in some way have only been won when we posed a threat, when we all started imagining how much better the world would be if we could abolish the State entirely rather than begging for scraps. But we need to remember, the moment they give anything up, they have already started plotting how they're going to take it back. Every reform either divides the oppressed, helps some while hurting others, or opens up pathways for entirely new techniques of domination and exploitation. Sometimes all three. Reforms are always designed to immobilize and institutionalize our movements. If we win a reform, it's not a moment to celebrate. It's a moment to prepare to protect ourselves against whatever is coming next.

We're like a novice at chess, going up against a master. We move a pawn out at an opportune moment and force our enemy's queen to retreat. We're ecstatic, seeing her run. In that moment, we think we might win. But we're forgetting how the game is actually played. If you don't make a single threatening move, your opponent could win without ever retreating. But most of the time, retreating is just a way to improve your position and go back on the attack.

And while it's important to celebrate the minor victories, our opponents have been playing this game for millennia. We have too, but we don't remember. Which is why it's so exciting the moment we rediscover that we can move forward and push them back. But simply moving forward isn't enough. They've been stockpiling their lessons. All their science, all their culture, all their history, is about learning how to keep us down.

If they pull back their queen, you better believe it's to angle for a counterattack.

The state perpetually prepares against revolution by giving us ineffective tools of resistance. When ruling institutions finally had to admit, in the twentieth century, that society would always be conflictual and uncontrollable, they shifted to a new paradigm of domination, in which resistance is allowed, but the tools of resistance that are readily available to people actually help the oppressive system update itself, repair itself, and become stronger.

Don't use respectability politics with a system that deserves no respect. Respectability politics is naïve, because those in power will never respect our desire to live healthy, free lives. They consider domination, exploitation, and greed respectable, and they systematically trample the dignity of the most marginalized members of society. Klee Benally, the Diné anarchist, describes how reformist elements at Standing Rock used the old divide between "good Indians" and "bad Indians" to be able to dialogue with power, even though it meant throwing others under the bus:

> The tactic of respectable appearances [...] becomes its own violence; it offers the flesh of Black Lives (who showed up in official and unofficial delegations to Standing Rock) and those *bad Indians* (militants, queers, etc.) in hopes of convincing the State that they are less disposable, they are the *good Indians*.[47]

Absolute nonviolence has always failed. In two previous books I have studied all the major victories claimed by proponents of exclusive nonviolence, as well as the statistical methodology they use to claim that nonviolence is more effective across the board. I revealed fatal flaws in that methodology, and in the case studies, I revealed how a victory was either a reform that was also favored by powerful elements of the ruling class because it increased their power without abolishing systems of oppression. Or it was a change brought about by a diversity of methods—including combative methods—that both the State and proponents of nonviolence later worked together to erase from the history.

The response has been to ignore the rebuttals and exclude them from the official conversation. The fact they haven't responded with factual analysis strongly suggests that they cannot.

47   Klee Benally, *No Spiritual Surrender: Indigenous Anarchy in Defense of the Sacred*, Detritus Books, 2023, p.100.

Not only is nonviolence ineffective, not only does it require the erasure of our memory in order to protect the comfort politics of its most influential practitioners, if nonviolence goes beyond a personal choice to become a strategic imposition on an entire movement, *it puts people in danger*. As Klee Benally writes, "Spiritually, mentally, physically pacifying the rage against colonial violence only serves to move us further into a neo-colonial dead-zone of historical trauma."[48]

To requote an anonymous criminal queer: **If we only defend, we end up with our backs against the wall.**

Only focusing on destruction will make us incapable of abolishing the State. The State also exists in our relationships, and we cannot will a relationship to disappear. Beings who share their survival on any level are always in relationship. We can attack the State indefinitely, without ever having the possibility of destroying it, if we refuse to cultivate relationships based on solidarity rather than domination. Yet some revolutionary currents, afraid of imposing a new solution on society, have fallen into a philosophical trap. Failing to see the difference between blueprints and imagination, between imposing something and cultivating it, is a failure to see the difference between anarchy and the State. Such a failure condemns us to turn struggle into a moral performance.

Imagination is a capacity, not a final destination, and if we do not cultivate our imagination, we will never be able to create other worlds or envision what healing looks like. Without our own imaginations, we can only adopt the imaginaries that the dominant culture produces for us. Without revolutionary

---

48   Benally, *No Spiritual Surrender*, p.105.

imagination, the State will always be able to define our future and redirect our movements.

Revolt is not predetermined by economic causes or any other mechanical force. We might revolt in times of poverty or times of economic growth, in times when the State that rules us feels powerful or feels weak. When exploitation and precarity are increasing, many people will turn towards even more oppressive systems. We always revolt in relation to the conditions we experience, but **we are always the ones who define our own experiences, identify our goals, and make the vital choice to revolt.** Without that step, there is no revolt.

We will repeat mistakes if we do not learn from them and remember them.

We will not remember our mistakes if we don't have continuity between one generation and the next.

We cannot build this intergenerational memory if we don't take care of one another.

Care, support, imagination, storytelling, and healing are some of the most important capacities a revolutionary movement needs to develop. Just as we need to abandon nonviolence and abandon the fetishization of combat that many armed vanguards have used to brand themselves as leaders, we need to forever leave behind the bland democratic framework of equality, which has only ever been a formalistic political equality used to cover up all the systems of oppression that are not codified but are every bit as real.

What we need to embrace without fear is difference—complementary differences and how they link us together—not as individuals made equal by a sheet of rights guaranteed by the State, but as beings in solidarity and mutual aid, each of us free to explore our own needs and talents and desires while understanding that we only survive together. Thus, the healer doesn't heal only herself, she heals so the community can be healthy. The fighter doesn't fight her own personal war, she risks herself so the whole can survive. The storyteller doesn't tell stories so he can become a famous author, he tells stories so that all those who came before him, who taught him, can live on through the next generations, sharing their experiences and creating a wealth of knowledge for everyone to grow from. And the mediator doesn't mediate to launch a career and live off of consulting fees after the prison system gets partially abolished, replaced by something just as bad. They mediate because all of us need to learn from our conflicts and our wounds so we can take care of one another and turn individual survival into collective abundance.

The list above offers a few compass points, and I'm excited to see where we can take them. I'm also excited by what feels like a growing ability to see failings that earlier generations had taken for granted, and that movements growing alongside us have a better perspective on.

Zarahn Southon recenters the importance of Indigenous resistance and a global anticolonial struggle, telling me what this has looked like for the Māori. He then directly addresses the need for white people to learn from and support those struggles without coopting them. "Europeans living within colonial societies" need to:

> ... first acknowledge the Indigenous specific to their area and learn about Indigenous resistance and colonial history. Secondly, to learn as much as possible about

working-class, anti-capitalist, and Indigenous struggle, but through the struggles of Black, Indigenous, and people of color (BIPOC) rather than the prism of European anarchists and intellectuals.

Lastly, building local community based upon face-to-face interaction is the only way for a mass movement and community to flourish. Kanohi ki te kanohi (face-to-face) interaction is at the heart of Māori tradition and present in today's Māori movement. No amount of social media interaction will surpass direct physical contact.

Our whakapapa—shared stories and histories of how we come into being, our relationships to one another and the environment—are vital for community building. The Ngāti Tūwharetoa rangatira (chief) Te Ngaehe Wanikau from my sister hapū of Ngāti Hikairo, several years ago travelled to a European environmental summit. He presented to the forum how we as Māori treat our mountains and rivers as living beings. He asked that we need to respect Pāpātuanuku our earth mother and care for her; he asked Europeans to do the same, to personify their mountains and rivers, however in their own unique way specific to Europe. It is a concept of stewardship that challenges the European concept of ownership. In Māori, no one owns the land, the land owns us.

This last point directly raises the question of spirituality, one which has emerged again and again throughout these pages. As I've argued elsewhere, every worldview, every belief system or paradigm—from scientific rationalism to Calvinism to Maoism to the traditional practices of the Māori—are imbued with their own spirituality. Some spiritual systems, like the Calvinism of one branch of my family, is explicitly at war with the world and hateful of the complexity of life. Others that claim not to have any spirituality at all, like scientific rationalism, can do even more damage when they constitute the dominant paradigm, because their harmful effects are often invisible and harder to challenge.

Every worldview entails its own spirituality because there are always questions that cannot be answered objectively, like which questions we choose to ask, which ones we don't, and how we frame them. We cannot avoid making choices that affirm how we understand ourselves, how we understand life and death and our relationship with the rest of the world, what we see as important, what we see as valid, what we see as healthy, and how we define health and happiness, freedom and fulfillment.

Revolutionaries who grow up in zones of whiteness, whatever their race or class, often adopt most features of the dominant spirituality while believing they are free of spiritual beliefs (confusing spirituality with religion, acknowledgment of relation with arbitrary and unexamined assumptions). And by zones of whiteness, I mean the corners of the world that have been most thoroughly colonized, where the institutions, the culture, and the spirituality of power that arose in Europe and conquered the rest of the world, is not only dominant but largely unquestioned. I believe that anarchists who fall into this pattern need to do better at understanding how colonialism operates and ask themselves, together with their friends, what is the shape of the world, and what is their place within it?

Curiously, the question of shape, of relation, can lead us directly to the question of organization, one of the other main problems that has been posed without any resolution throughout this book. We can find many lessons on how *not* to organize ourselves, but how *do* we organize ourselves, both at a more continental or global scale, and for those of us who do not come from traditionally stateless societies, at the local scale as well?

There is plenty of theorizing, and analysis of our recent failings, that attempts to push this question further.

The underground book *Here at the Center of the World in Revolt* suggests that we will only escape the trap of authoritarian or self-defeating organizations when we learn to look at the world in another way, understanding that every single point is the center of the world, and embracing the sort of decentralized networks that demands of us.[49]

Void Network, in their text "Introduction to Anarchist Pluralism,"[50] strike out in a similar direction, calling for the acceptance of contradictions:

> To coordinate our differences, to unite not in common agreements but in parallel disagreements, in anti-hegemonic strategies and methodologies that complement each other. To create an organic culture, not an organization, thousands of collectives, not a singular political party—a world of freedom that includes all possible free worlds.

One of the deepest features of colonial culture causes us to confuse the question of organization from the moment we approach it. In classical anarchism, the debate has often been

49 Lev Zlodey and Jason Radegas, *Here at the Center of the World in Revolt*, 2014: https://theanarchistlibrary.org/library/lev-zlodey-jason-radegas-here-at-the-center-of-a-world-in-revolt (accessed April 20, 2024.

50 Void Network, "Introduction to Anarchist Pluralism," Athens: 2023. The translation was provided to me by the authors and is not yet published in English.

an exhausting distraction, a battle between partisans of formality or informality, proponents of one organizational type or another. *Organization, Continuity, and Community* is the text I wrote to distill the inspirations and disappointments I've experienced through all the years I've been in struggle, as well as the defeats and lessons of those I've learned the most from. In it, I try to share a different approach:

> Once we understand it strictly as a tool, we no longer ask whether formal or informal organization is better, nor do we understand them to exist in some absurd ideological competition. For each task, we look for the best tool. If we are lacking a tool that we need in our struggle, we create it. We are not adherents of the hammer and not the fork; we wouldn't sit down to eat spaghetti with a hammer. Being a partisan of one or another kind of organization is equally absurd.
>
> At this point, we can propose a more developed imaginary: organization is the process of generating collective bodies, bodies beyond the individual. This is where a consciousness of the chaotic nature of the universe becomes unavoidable: these collective bodies already exist and have always existed. The lies of liberalism and capitalist alienation have made us feel like sovereign individuals (or dependent, subordinate ones), but those individuals do not exist. We only exist within a network of relations. All this is to say that to organize ourselves is to transform and structure the collective webs that already exist. We are already organized under capitalism, but it is a kind of organization that makes solidarity and struggle almost impossible.

The result of this approach is to understand all our organizational efforts as occurring within an ecosystem of struggle.

Our goal should never be to dominate that ecosystem, because by doing so we would only destroy it. Instead, we should organize ourselves in a way to add to the richness of the overall ecosystem, filling up niches that are abandoned or neglected, and finding ways to act that are complementary with others who also make up the ecosystem. And when we can't work together, taking space rather than trying to eliminate those we are in conflict with. Once we choose to embrace the eco-systemic nature of this world we share, and this struggle, we can see that we only survive together. Integrating mutual aid to that degree, in our actions and also in our understanding of who we are, maybe we'll have a chance of surviving after all, one generation after the next, passing on what we've learned, and always learning new things.

I've shared what I can, though none of these conversations are over. And I've pointed out a few paths I find particu-larly promising, but maybe you've found even better ones to explore. The only thing left to say, perhaps, is *we remember, and we'll hold each other close until we meet again.*

Recommended Readings:
A Library Of Our Experiences

Chapter 1

Anonymous, *Unfinished Acts*

Anonymous (documentary), *Touch the Sky: Stories, Subversions, and Complexities of Ferguson*

Anonymous, 2010, *"Each Cop Hides a Secret: It's Easy to Attack"*

CASA Collective, *Teaching Rebellion: Stories from the Grassroots Mobilization in Oaxaca*

CrimethInc, "How (Not) to Abolish the Police

CrimethInc, *From Democracy to Freedom*

Fray Baroque and Tegan Eanelli, *Queer Ultraviolence: Bash Back! Anthology*

jimmy cooper and Lyn Corelle (eds.), *Make the Golf Course a Public Sex Forest*

Kimathi Mohammed, *Organization and Spontaneity*

Kuwasi Balagoon, *A Soldier's Story*

Lev Zlodey and Jason Radegas, *Here at the Center of the World in Revolt*

Lorenzo Kom'boa Ervin, *Anarchism and the Black Revolution*

Modibo Kadalie, *Internationalism, Pan-Africanism, and the Struggle of Social Classes*

Peter Gelderloos, *How Nonviolence Protects the State*

Peter Gelderloos, *The Failure of Nonviolence*

Russell Maroon Shoatz, *The Dragon and the Hydra*

Sagris, Schwarz, Void Network (eds.), *We Are an Image from the Future: The Greek Revolt of December 2008*

William C. Anderson, *The Nation on No Map; Black Anarchism and Abolition*

Chapter 2

CrimethInc, *Green Scared? Some Lessons from the FBI Crackdown on Eco-Activists*

Do or Die: Voices from Earth First! archived at libcom.org

Elli King, *Listen: The Story of the People at Taku Wakan Tipi and the Reroute of Highway 55 Or The Minnehaha Free State*

John Severino, "With Land, Without the State: Anarchy in Wallmapu" and "The Intensification of Independence in Wallmapu"

Klee Benally, *No Spiritual Surrender: Indigenous Anarchy in Defense of the Sacred*

Neal Shirley and Saralee Stafford, *Dixie Be Damned: 300 Years of Insurrection in the American South*

Peter Gelderloos, *The Solutions Are Already Here: Strategies for Ecological Revolution from Below*

Peter Gelderloos, *Anarchy Works*

Peter Gelderloos, "Whiteness Is a War Measure"

Will Potter, *Green Is the New Red: An Insider's Account of a Social Movement Under Siege*

Chapter 3

Anonymous, *Secrets and Lies*, Ungrateful Hyenas Editions, 2022

Bash Back! News, "We Cut Our Teeth on Each Other"

Cindy Milstein (ed.), *Rebellious Mourning*

Cindy Milstein (ed.), *There Is Nothing So Whole As a Broken Heart: Mending the World As Jewish Anarchists*

Dean Spade, *Mutual Aid*

Fourth Wave: London Feminist Activists, "When Abusers Hijack the Language of Feminism," *Freedom News*, September 2018

Leah Lakshmi Piepzna-Samarasinha, *Care Work: Dreaming Disability Justice*

Mariame Kaba, *We Do This 'Til We Free Us: Abolitionist Organizing and Transforming Justice*

Peter Gelderloos, *Worshiping Power: An Anarchist View of Early State Formation*

Peter Gelderloos, *Organization, Continuity, Community*

Ricard de Vargas Golarons (ed.), *Salvador Puig Antich: Collected Writings on Repression and Resistance in Franco's Spain*

Saidiya Hartman, *Lose Your Mother*

The Tilted Scales Collective, *A Tilted Guide to Being a Defendant and Representing Radicals: A Guide for Lawyers and Movements*

Void Network, "Introduction to Anarchist Pluralism"

Volin, *The Unknown Revolution*

Zoe Samudzi and William Anderson, *As Black As Resistance: Finding the Conditions for Liberation*